EASY STATISTICS IN PSYCHOLOGY

WITHDRAWN

EASY STATISTICS
IN PSYCHOLOGY
A BPS GUIDE

MARK FORSHAW

BPS Blackwell

© 2007 by Blackwell Publishing Ltd
A BPS Blackwell book

BLACKWELL PUBLISHING
350 Main Street, Malden, MA 02148-5020, USA
9600 Garsington Road, Oxford OX4 2DQ, UK
550 Swanston Street, Carlton, Victoria 3053, Australia

The right of Mark Forshaw to be identified as the Author of this Work has been asserted in accordance with the UK Copyright, Designs, and Patents Act 1988.

First published 2007 by the British Psychological Society and Blackwell Publishing Ltd

1   2007

Library of Congress Cataloging-in-Publication Data
Forshaw, Mark.
    Easy statistics in psychology : a BPS guide / Mark Forshaw.
        p. cm.
    Includes bibliographical references and index.
    ISBN 978-1-4051-3956-4 (hardcover : alk. paper) – ISBN 978-1-4051-3957-1 (pbk. : alk. paper)
1. Psychometrics. 2. Psychology–Statistical methods. I. Title.
    BF39.F67 2008
    150.1´5195–dc22
                        2007022953

A catalogue record for this title is available from the British Library.

Set in 10 on 12.5pt Rotis Serif
by Prepress Projects Ltd, Algo Business Centre, Glenearn Road, Perth PH2 0NJ, UK
Printed and bound in Singapore
by C.O.S. Printers Pte Ltd

The publisher's policy is to use permanent paper from mills that operate a sustainable forestry policy, and which has been manufactured from pulp processed using acid-free and elementary chlorine-free practices. Furthermore, the publisher ensures that the text paper and cover board used have met acceptable environmental accreditation standards.

For further information on
BPS Blackwell, visit our website:
www.bpsblackwell.com

The British Psychological Society's free Research Digest e-mail service rounds up the latest research and relates it to your syllabus in a user-friendly way. To subscribe go to www. researchdigest.org.uk or send a blank e-mail to subscribe-rd@lists.bps.org.uk

CONTENTS

PREFACE

Before you start reading this book, there's something that you should know. Some years ago, I was at school, at a parents' evening, and my mathematics teacher told my mother and father that I was not capable of passing the examination that was coming up in 18 months or so. Thankfully, in my final year at school, I was fortunate enough to be taught by a different person entirely, who really made a difference. In just one year, she taught my class everything we needed to know. I was also working hard at home to understand what I had to, and one week before the examination it all clicked into place. I passed, and not just barely, but with a very respectable grade. The moral of this tale is that you need two things to figure out numbers and what to do with them: a good teacher and some determination. Don't give up.

Then, at university, I failed one of my two statistics examinations, and my psychology studies would have been over unless I passed the re-sits. Again, with some hard work and preparation, I got through. As you can see, I'm not a statistics genius. I am not naturally gifted with numbers, and in fact have always been a 'words' person instead, but I found a way around it.

Over the years, I have taught thousands of students about psychological statistics and research methods, and I have learned something new with each new group of students, without exception. When I figured out a new way to understand issues in statistics, I passed this on to my students, and it helped them. That's where this book comes from. I sincerely hope that it can help you.

One common complaint that a psychology student can make about statistics is that they can't cope because they say that they are 'not a numbers person'. Well, neither am I, as I said. However, claiming that you are not a 'numbers person' is lying to yourself a little. Ask yourself what a number actually is. Here's one: 3. Now, this is also a word: three. The figure

3 is simply another way of expressing an idea, which can be presented as a word too. The Romans represented it like this: III. In Dutch it's *drie*, in French *trois*, in Spanish *tres*, in German *drei*. In Swahili it is *tatu*. However, it's just an idea being expressed in each case.

Now, prepare yourself for a shock. *Statistics is not about numbers.* Honestly, it's not. It's about *ideas*. In fact, most mathematicians will tell you the same. Mathematics is like philosophy. Of course, we use special symbols to put those ideas onto paper because it is useful to do so and avoids confusion and uses less space. The moment we use those symbols, some people scream and run away. That's why, in this book, I avoid using those symbols whenever possible. Once you understand the ideas, you can start to tackle the symbols, but I really think that the ideas are the most important thing of all.

In this book, you will learn about the main statistics you need to know about in an average psychology degree, and in a way that you can cope with. I have tried to make things as easy as possible, and have made frequent use of analogies. By comparing something you don't understand to something that you do, there's a good chance that you'll start to see the point of it all. Therefore, instead of formulae and equations, I'm telling you about cakes and vacuum cleaners and spotlights. There you go: read on and you will discover why I can see a cake in an analysis of variance. Of course, if you don't understand cakes, I can recommend a good bakery...

ACKNOWLEDGEMENTS

My thanks to Laura Fletcher, for the illustrations. She obligingly translated my rough sketches into real artwork, and at extremely short notice. Dr Peter Watson, statistician and all-round cake and biscuit connoisseur of the University of Cambridge, checked this book for accuracy, with his typical good grace and humour; any mistakes or misinterpretation that remain are, of course, entirely my fault. I am grateful to my colleagues Hugh Coolican and David Clark-Carter for conversations about statistics that I have had with them which have sparked off new ideas. I would like to thank Sarah Bird and Will Maddox (who helped to start me on the path of writing this book), and Andrew McAleer and Elizabeth Johnston who took over this project at BPS Blackwell. I have known Andrew for some years now, and I am still bemused by his ability to listen to me gibber on manically about book ideas without losing patience. Finally, I am grateful to Amanda Crowfoot, for helping to refine some of my analogies, for talking things through with me, even though she's neither a statistician nor a psychologist, and for generally finding me worthwhile.

Dr Mark Forshaw
May 2007

AN INTRODUCTION TO MEASURING THINGS

All of statistics is based upon numbers which represent ideas, as I suggested in the Preface. Those numbers are also measurements, taken from the world, or derived from experiments we have undertaken. Therefore, the building blocks of statistics are measurements. It is, therefore, important that you understand the very principles upon which measurements are taken.

Σ LEVELS OF MEASUREMENT

Whenever you measure something, you measure it in a particular way. Some measurements are more sensitive than others, and this is very important for us to understand because it underpins the statistical procedures that we employ. Some data come in a particular form, and that's that. However, occasionally we can dictate the nature of the data depending upon the measurements we take. Therefore, it is crucial that we are familiar with different types of measurement and different types of data, primarily because we can, in theory, change the very nature of what we are studying if we measure and test in different ways.

You are probably confused by that statement, so let us work backwards, and then you can read it again later, and you'll see what it means.

There are four basic types of data, or levels of measurement, as we call them. These are called *nominal, ordinal, interval* and *ratio.* Data can only be of one type, although statisticians and psychologists might actually argue sometimes about which category certain data fall into.

Nominal data are in the forms of categories or names of things. In fact, sometimes nominal data are referred to as categorical. Nominal data are generally seen as the least informative, and nominal measurements are the least sensitive of those that we can take. Nominal data are essentially in the form of labels. You can't perform standard mathematical operations on them. For example, bus routes often have numbers attached to them. However, although the Number 10 takes the same route every day, it doesn't actually go half as far as the Number 20. The Number 15 is not 50% more expensive to travel on than the Number 10. The Number 658 isn't the best bus of all, even if it's the highest number that the bus company uses. The numbers are only codes. Other common examples include the numbers on football players' shirts, postal or zip codes, and people's names. I can count up how many Sarahs in a certain population, and I can count how many Janes there are, but I can't divide Sarahs by Janes, and I can't work out the average name by adding them up and dividing by the number of numbers. A common example of this type or error is when students ask a statistical package to automatically work out the average of a set of scores. If your scores are simply labels for different groups of people, this is meaningless. That is, imagine that you have coded men as 1 and women as 2. If you work out the averages of your scores, you might discover that the mean sex of participants is 1.4. Now what on earth does that mean? The mean sex of a participant in your sample is, it seems, halfway between male and female, but ever so slightly more male. There is an old joke that runs like this: if I put my head in the refrigerator and my feet in a bowl of hot water, my temperature *on average* is just about right. No? A friend and I are out walking when we come to a junction where we can go one of three ways. There is a path to the left, one to the right, and one in the middle. Unbeknown to us, only the middle path leads where we want to go. But, I take the left path, he takes the right, and, *statistically*, that means that *on average* we took the middle path and got to our intended destination. No? Right: I think you get the point here about nominal data. This type of data is very basic, and there is not much you can do with it.

If we put the types of data in order of their sensitivity and usefulness, then the next one in line is called ordinal data. This is pretty much what it sounds like. Ordinal data tell you what order things are in, but not a lot more. Therefore, world chess rankings are ordinal. The order of finishers in a race (without their race times) is also ordinal. Now, you can probably see why this kind of data is better than that which is nominal, but still carries some strong limits. After all, knowing what order things are in is good, but knowing how far apart they are is better. I might beat you in a race today, so that I finish first and you finish second. If I beat you by only one second, you would be right to suggest that this is not necessarily very meaningful, and that on another day you might be able to finish first instead. However, if I beat you by minutes, or even hours, that would probably give you a good idea of who was the better runner. Ordinal data fall short of giving us this crucial information. This leads us onto interval data.

Interval data are measured in such a way that one does know the distance (if you like) between points on our scale. We not only know the order of the finishers of the race now, but also their actual race times, which allows us much more scope to understand the relationships between things we can measure in such a way. Many data used in psychology are interval in nature. The classic example of this kind of data is temperature in degrees Celsius. The difference between 10 and 20 is the same amount as the difference between 20 and 30, and so on. However, there is one characteristic missing, which sets interval data apart from ratio data. The Celsius scale does not have a true zero. Zero degrees does not mean 'no temperature'. It is simply a marker. For convenience, we chose the freezing point of water to correspond with this point on the scale. But, we have to bear in mind that there is still a temperature going on! Some people in the past have asked me about 'absolute zero' on the Kelvin scale of temperature. This corresponds to −273 degrees centigrade. It's basically the coldest it is possible for something to be. Now, the thing that is important here is that absolute zero is a true zero, because the Kelvin scale is an index of heat energy present in a substance. No heat energy is zero degrees Kelvin. There really is no heat energy present at all, which is why it can't get any colder. Kelvin, therefore, is a *ratio* level of measurement, which we can now turn to.

Ratio data are the 'best' kind of data of all, at least in terms of sensitivity in statistical testing. Ratio data are interval data measured on a scale with a true zero. The number of items recalled in a memory test is ratio data; it is possible to get zero correct, if you don't remember anything. Furthermore, when you get 2 correct, it is half as much as someone who gets 4. There is a perfect mathematical relationship between the items. For reasons I won't go into, this fits very neatly into a whole bunch of statistical tests we have invented over the years. One nice and easy reason for you to ponder is that ratio data have a tendency to end up being normally distributed, at least more often than the other forms of data, some of which actually can't ever be! Therefore, given that we have developed our tests to compare distributions of scores with approximately normal shapes, ratio data are most likely to provide that.

Σ MEASURES OF CENTRAL TENDENCY

Staring at sets of numbers can, from time to time, be quite useful, but there's a limit to that usefulness. Also, the larger the sets become the more difficult it is to get any sense of their properties by 'eyeballing', as it is called. Therefore, we need some way of characterising and summarising data, and that is why we have developed the descriptive statistics known as measures of central tendency. Why 'central tendency'? The answer is that, in this case, 'central' refers to average, in the sense that numbers tend to cluster, and that clustering we can call a 'centre'. Note that I said 'tend'... Hence central tendency. Measures of central tendency are simply ways of telling us what the numbers in a set are like, on average.

There are three main kinds of average, and although the mean tends to be used the most, the mode and the median are also handy at times. Sometimes, you cannot use a mean, for example because it completely misrepresents the data. We can examine the detail of three the types of measure now.

Mean

The mean is the kind of measure of central tendency that most people are referring to when they use the word 'average'. Simply, you summate all of the numbers in a set, and then divide by the number of numbers in the set. Mathematically, this takes all of the numbers into account, and there is a kind of 'tug-o'-war' that occurs in the formula. Numbers pull each other back and forth, but in the end the mean settles at the point where most of the values lie. A very high or very low number will not influence the mean greatly because the mean is normally found where the majority of values are to be found. The mean is best used when a set of numbers are normally distributed (that is, where most people score in the middle, and a few people score very highly or very low), so you should always check the frequency distribution before you automatically calculate the mean. If the distribution doesn't look like this, then it might be a good idea to avoid relying on the mean.

The mean should not be used when the data are categorical. It doesn't make sense to calculate the average sex of your participants, when you have labelled men as 1 and women as 2. You'd probably end up with a mean of somewhere around 1.5. Of course, it's nonsensical. What sex is 1.5? Additionally, don't calculate means when you appear to have a bimodal distribution, that is where there seem to be two peaks of scores (Figure 1.1). If there is a bunch of low scores and a bunch of high scores, with virtually nothing in the middle, the mean is not going to adequately depict the scores. What happens in this case is that the mean ends up being somewhere in the middle. Think about it: how can you have an average score which no-one actually achieves? It's a contradiction in terms. The

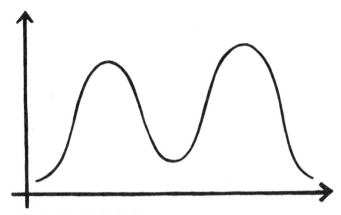

Figure 1.1 A largely bimodal distribution.

average must tell you what most scores are like, not what none or a few are.

Mode

A mode is used in a few rare circumstances. All you have to do to identify the mode is look for the most commonly occurring number in your set. Not only is this a good way to eyeball small sets of data, it also works well for categorical data. If you want to know which of three choices of steak sauce is the most popular, you can simply count up the numbers of people choosing each. The most commonly occurring is the most popular steak sauce, and precisely because it is the most popular sauce it also is what the average diner will choose, if you like. This is no more than common sense!

You can't use the mode if there are lots of decimals in your data, or if there are many different numbers and none the same. Imagine a dataset containing numbers to five decimal places, such as 0.00452. The same number might never occur twice, in which case there can't be a distinct mode. Either that, or in a dataset of 140 different numbers there are really 140 modes! Since the purpose of a measure of central tendency is to summarise the essential property of a set of numbers, having to list them all over again hardly works.

In fact, the mode is extremely limited. It also won't do the job when there are just a small number of identical data, and many other, different scores. In the following dataset, 3 is the mode, but it really doesn't represent the set properly because most of the other figures are much higher: 2, 2, 3, 3, 3, 3, 38, 45, 46, 48, 50, 55, 65, 71, 71, 72, 73, 74, 75, 80, 99.

Median

The median is a very simple measure of central tendency to work out because it doesn't involve any calculation. All you have to do is put the numbers in order of magnitude and then find the one right in the middle. With an even number of scores, you have to choose halfway between the two scores nearest the centre. Nothing more, nothing less. This can be a very useful descriptive statistic, especially when you have some extreme scores or outliers which you don't want to trim out of your data, for whatever reason. The median is not affected by extreme scores because it is based upon finding whatever is in the middle of the set, making the tails of the distribution almost irrelevant.

For example, let us take these numbers: 1, 1, 5, 6, 8, 9, 10, 24, 25. The median is 8. Now, imagine what would happen if the lowest score was now 0 and the highest score was 11,475. That is, 0, 1, 5, 6, 8, 9, 10, 24, 11,475. The median is still 8! The means for the two sets vary massively, however. The first has a mean of 9.89, and the second a mean of 1282. Here's an example not only of the reason why medians are helpful statistics, but also why means of small samples can be very misleading, since extreme scores can really pull the mean away from where it might more sensibly lie. The mode in the first set of figures, by the way, is 1, since that number occurs twice, and the others only once each. So, for the second set we have no mode (or nine modes, depending on how you look at it), a mean of 1282 and a median of 8. Quite different, aren't they? Since the whole purpose of descriptive statistics are to describe the data, it isn't difficult to identify which is the most accurate at doing so.

Σ | NORMAL DISTRIBUTION

When you collect data, it is possible to look at the scores you have in terms of a frequency distribution. A frequency distribution is simply a way of seeing how the data are spread out along the range of scores. If you gave people a visuo-spatial test of reasoning, it might be possible to score as little as zero, and as much as 100, for example. We might want to know just how many people score highly, or how many people score below average, and so on. A frequency distribution can reveal this. It is common to plot such a distribution using a bar graph and categories of data, for example 0–10, 11–20, 21–30, and so on. In a frequency distribution, the number of people gaining scores in that particular band are shown by the height of a bar on the bar graph.

Frequency distributions can vary considerably in their shapes. The most basic form, and the most useless for statisticians and psychologists, is what we would call a monomial distribution. This is where everyone achieves exactly the same score. Sometimes, certain data are what we called binomially distributed. This time, people either get one score or they get another. Binomial distributions of data should be a warning sign that you are really dealing not with a continuous variable, but rather a categorical one. If everyone seems to score either high or low, and little else, then to all intents and purposes you should not consider the data to be spread across a scale.

Most scores that we collect in psychology are likely to be distributed normally. This is set by definition, since a normal distribution means a distribution which occurs as a norm, i.e. what normally happens. Normal distributions have a clearly defined shape. They look like a bell, which is why they are also called 'bell curves'. They have a hump in the middle, and small tails at each extreme, with scores trailing off steadily towards those 'tails'. What this means is quite simple: most people are found to be scoring in the middle range of collected data, a few people achieve very high scores, and a few people achieve very low scores. The average score is right in the middle of the hump, and this doesn't matter whether you use the mean, the mode, or the median as your measure of central tendency.

The possession of normally distributed data is an ideal situation for most statistical analyses. It is what we call an *assumption* of many statistical tests. You might legitimately ask why this is so important. Well, without boring or confusing you with the fine detail, suffice it to say that that most parametric, inferential, statistical tests are constructed to be fed normally distributed data. If your data aren't normally distributed, you will run up against problems. It's the same as cars which run on diesel fuel instead of petrol. If you want to know why you have to use diesel, you'll have to understand engineering, but most diesel vehicle owners simply accept that the engine was made that way and get on with the process of filling up with the right kind of fuel. A car with the wrong fuel in the tank is a bit like a statistical test fed the wrong kind of data. It won't work.

Normally distributed data are to be found all over the natural world. Height, weight, blood pressure, finger length, width and depth of rivers are all normally distributed. Most people are of 'average' height, and there are a small number of very tall and very short people. Most people are of 'average' weight, with a few very heavy and very light ones making up the tails of the distribution. The same goes for the other variables I mentioned above, and literally millions of others, including psychological ones such as vocabulary score, intelligence and problem-solving ability.

The Case of the Normal Distribution

When you have a perfectly normally distributed set of data, conforming exactly to the classic bell curve, something rather special happens to the measures of central tendency. They converge to the same point, which is the peak of the hump in the middle of the distribution, or, the vertical axis of symmetry, as you can see in Figure 1.2. That is, they are all the same. In a perfect normal distribution, the mean, mode and median are exactly the same number.

Now, this is something that is worth remembering for the future. As you'll see elsewhere in this book, and beyond, statisticians have a tendency to be a little obsessed with normal distributions. They base so much of what they do on them, and researchers almost pray for them to arise in their data. This is one of the reasons. It makes life so much easier when you don't have to make the choice between measures of central tendency. You don't have to know which one is best, or carefully examine the data to work it out, because they are all the same. Oh, and here's a little tip. One way to quickly check if a dataset is likely to be normally distributed is to get SPSS or some other software to calculate the three main measures of

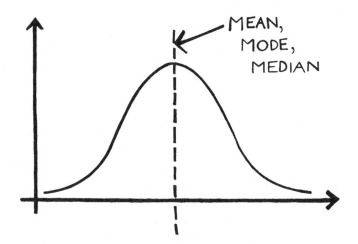

Figure 1.2 Measures of central tendency in a normal distribution.

central tendency for you, and to see how close to each other they are. If they are only a whisker away from each other, there's a very high chance that you have normally distributed data. Don't forget to plot a frequency graph, however, to check the shape visually.

There are other ways to test for normality. We can calculate coefficients which tell us about the size of the tails of the distribution in relation to the hump in the middle, how pointy or flat or asymmetrical the distribution is. If we do this, rather than just looking at the shape of the curve on a graph, we can be that bit more certain of what it is we are dealing with. In statistics, we almost always prefer a number over a picture. Pictures can tell us that something might be wrong, whereas a statistical test can tell us just how wrong, and how likely it is that we are right when we say it is wrong! (Sorry if you are confused. All I mean to convey to you is that just because something looks wrong doesn't mean that it is, and just because something appears right isn't enough to feel confident that it is.)

There are two main tests of normality, and these are the Kolmogorov–Smirnov and Shapiro–Wilk tests. SPSS will compute them very easily for you, and what they essentially do is compare your data with an hypothesised or 'idealised' normal distribution and look for a difference. They give you a probability value like other statistical tests, but this time you are looking for high probabilities rather than low ones. A value of P greater than 0.05 indicates that there is no difference between your data and a normal distribution. That's a good thing, because if there's no difference, that means that you have, to all intents and purposes, a normal distribution! However, if the value of P is less than 0.05, your data are significantly different from a normal set, which of course means that they are not normal.

One word of warning. When you have very small samples (less than about ten), tests of normality are generally very insensitive to violations of normality. So, rather ironically, tiny samples tend to pass the normality test when in fact they aren't normal, and it's almost impossible for them to be normal anyway because there aren't enough numbers present to make up a normal curve!

The problems that such tests can bring about make many statisticians avoid them altogether, choosing instead to use 'rules of thumb'. They differ on these, and there are no official regulations, as it were! Look at the statistics for skew and kurtosis that SPSS gives you, and look at the standard errors that come next to them. Compare each statistic with its standard error. If the statistic is more than twice the standard error you should think of this as indicating a problem with non-normality. Well, that's what Coolican (2004) suggests. However, some say that you needn't worry about skew unless the statistic is greater than plus or minus one. Some say that as long as skewness is acceptable you needn't worry too much about kurtosis at all. Furthermore, most of this debate is about enabling the statistician to choose between different tests to use: the parametric and non-parametric ones (which you'll come across later in the book). Therefore, it is not uncommon for statisticians simply to run both tests on the data and then compare them. If they don't really differ, the chances are you have a result you can be sure of.

2

VARIANCE AND MORE

Any set of scores can be described in terms of its variance. It is a characteristic of data, and a very important one. If you can understand what variance is, you have the key to opening all of the other doors to comprehension of statistical tests in general.

Let us take an easy set of scores: 1, 2, 3. Just three numbers. Now, you'll notice that these are three different numbers. What do we mean by that? We mean that 1 is not the same as 2, 2 is not the same as 3, and 3 is not the same as 1. So, the numbers are *spread out*. The next question we have to ask ourselves is what we mean by spread out. There has to be some benchmark against which we measure the amount of spread. An easy way to do this is to see how spread out the scores are in relation to the average score in the set. The average of 1, 2, and 3 is 2. So, 1 is 1 away from 2, 2 is 0 away from 2, and 3 is 1 away from 2. In other words, we now have three numbers based on the differences from the mean of the set: 1, 0 and −1. Can you see why we have −1? Well, it is because 2 minus 3 gives −1. You will notice that if we simply add these numbers up, we get zero. That's no use in telling us how spread out the scores are. We can see that the spread is greater than zero! Also, you might like to try this with another set of numbers. You'll find that you always get zero! So, we take the simplest solution, and square all of the numbers. So, 1×1 is 1, 0×0 is 0, and -1×-1 is 1. If we add these up, we get 2. Then, we divide by 3, giving us the average amount by which the numbers deviate. So, 2 divided by 3 is 0.667. That's the variance! Many statistical tests, especially, as you might guess, analysis of variance, depend upon this to pick up trends in data.

Now we can start to move a little forward and deal with another very important descriptive statistic, the *standard deviation*. If you understand variance, then standard deviation is easy to define, as it is simply the positive square root of the variance. That's all. Simply take the variance, and find its square root and you have the standard deviation. Largely, you need to take a square root to remove the squares you applied earlier in calculating the variance. It's a little more complicated than this, but this should help you to remember the relationship between the two statistics.

So what is the standard deviation for, and why is it standard? I hope that you are asking these two questions, because it should now be obvious why it is called a 'deviation'. After all, it's a measure of 'spread-outness', which is my made-up word for deviation! These two questions are best answered together; we use standard deviations to give us a general idea of the spread of scores that means something no matter what the measure, and they are 'standard' because they relate to a standard normal curve. For most research and subsequent analysis, our ideal distribution of scores in a set is a normal one. A standard deviation for a set of scores tells us how spread out or squashed up they are, but because it is based on a normal curve it also tells us what proportion of scores fall between the mean and one, two, three standard deviations and so on. Then not only might we know that a person has scored one standard deviation above the mean, but we know what percentage of people also score between the mean and one standard deviation, or two, or three. It gives our scores *context*, if you like.

It's all about area under the curve, really. I remember having to learn to use calculus at school. We spent what seems like months and months on it. It probably was that much, since it's quite a complicated thing. At the time, my biggest problem was that I really didn't understand *why* you'd want to measure the area under a curve. It was a real sticking point for me, and I don't remember the teacher being able to give me a satisfactory answer. Then, not so many years ago, I suddenly realised it for myself when I started to really get my head around normal distributions and standard scores and probability curves. So, if you too learned calculus and didn't know why, stay tuned...

By definition, a normal curve is normal. It has a specified shape, and the idealised normal distribution is what it is. Of course, real data usually only approximate to this, but that's neither here nor there at the moment. The normal curve is like a mountain, and the top of the mountain is the mean of the set of scores. Either side of this, an exactly equal area is bounded by the curve and the horizontal axis. The distribution is symmetrical. You can fold it over using the mean as the folding point, and it will match exactly. The area between the mean and one standard deviation includes a set percentage of scores: always. As I said, this is based upon an exactly normal distribution, but that's the best we can get. So, here's the specific information.

34.13% of scores (area under the curve) are to be found between the mean and one standard deviation from it. It doesn't matter which side of the mean that one standard deviation is, because it's a symmetrical distribution. You just need to be aware of it by, when appropriate, sticking a minus or plus in front of the number. Of course, this means that 68.26% of scores are to be found in the area cut off by one standard deviation either side of the mean. Easy, isn't it? Two standard deviations from the mean on one side cut off 47.72% of the area under the curve. Two on each side gives you 95.44% of the scores bounded. Finally, three standard deviations on one side of the mean cut off 49.87% of scores. So, yes, we double it again, and 99.74% of the scores are included in the area bounded by three standard deviations each side of the mean. How do we get 100%, you ask? Well, basically, you don't. The tails don't touch the horizontal axis. That's because a real normal distribution has infinite tails. They *never* touch the axis. So, if you want the remaining 0.26% of the scores, you'll need to travel all the way along the line forever. But, after all, what's 0.26%? Not worth worrying about really. This is why I am not going to tell you why normal distributions have infinite tails. It's too complicated, and you'll almost certainly never *need* to know why.

This is all very interesting, but completely theoretical, as it refers to hypothetical normal distributions, the like of which we don't see very often in real studies. You'd be right to wonder what standard deviations tell us about real distributions of scores. Well, I had to tell you about the normal ones before I moved on to the subject of non-normal ones, because you have to learn to walk before you run. So, let's now deal with how to interpret standard deviations in real data that we have collected.

We need to understand standard deviations in context in order for them to tell us something useful. By context, I mean the other characteristics of the sample of data, that is the range and the mean. When we've collected data, we know what the lowest score is, and the highest score, and we have calculated the mean and standard deviation (usually using a software package such as SPSS). To make it easy, let's imagine that the lowest score is 0 and the highest 10, and the mean is in the middle, i.e. 5. now we must look at the standard deviation. *Always* do this when you are looking at scores. Never ignore the standard deviation, since it's a clue to how normal or non-normal your distribution is. Knowing that will tell you if you have very wonky data that are at worst useless and at best need some fiddling about with. If the standard deviation of a set of scores with the characteristics above is very high, then it means that lots of scores deviate wildly from the mean, giving us a very flat distribution, or possibly even a binomial distribution. In our case, a standard deviation of more than about 3 is likely to be highly problematic. Figure 2.1 shows this.

As you can see, neither of the distributions in Figure 2.1 and Figure 2.2 is anywhere near normal. The spread is very great in the first one. The first of these is also what we call a *platykurtic* distribution. Conversely, what does it tell us if the standard deviation is very low? With our scale of 1 to 10 and a mean of 5, a standard deviation of less than 1 is usually something to worry about. Basically, the standard deviation tells us that the scores are very much clustered around the mean. The tails are virtually non-existent. As you can see from Figure 2.2, the distribution is again far from normal, and is a 'spike'. We call this a *leptokurtic* distribution.

Statistical tests vary in the tolerance that they have for non-normal distributions. Parametric tests such as the independent *t*-test or analysis of variance really don't work very well at all if you feed them non-normal data. That's one reason why you must always look carefully at data before you analyse them. Always check the standard deviation in relation to the range and the mean, and plot a frequency distribution to see what the data actually look like. The more you do this, the more comfortable you get with the relationship between the graph, the standard deviation and the other characteristics of the data. You can even, after a while, skip the graph in most cases and use just the numbers to generate a mental picture of your own.

Following on from standard deviations, there is another measure of dispersion that you need to be familiar with, although, to be honest,

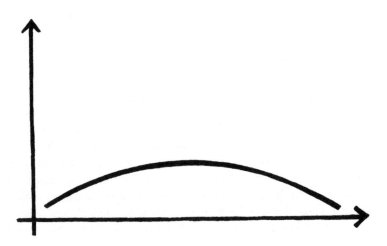

Figure 2.1 A population of scores with a very high standard deviation.

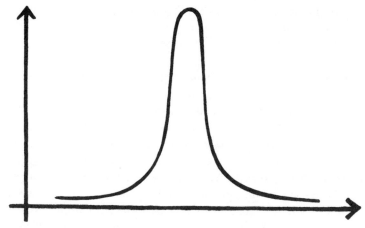

Figure 2.2 A population of scores with a very low standard deviation.

you'll rarely use directly. It is called the z-score. So why do you need to know about it? The answer is that sometimes you *will* need to use it, and sometimes you will read articles that, for good reasons, cite z-scores, and you ought to be ready should that happen.

In many ways, z-scores are just a version of the standard deviation adapted for a particular purpose. They are not hard to understand if you have followed everything I have just told you about the standard deviation. In fact, most confusion arises because people forget why z-scores tell us anything over and above the standard deviation.

Quite simply, we use z-scores to compare individual scores in a set in terms of the number of standard deviations they are from the mean, rather than their absolute values. So, if I tell you that I got 15 on a multiple-choice vocabulary test, that in itself doesn't tell you much. Someone else got 10. So what? Now, if I tell you that my score was exactly the mean, and the other score was one standard deviation below it, you know that I am average and the other person below average (although not dramatically below). My z-score is zero. The other person's z-score is −1. Because you also know the properties of a normal distribution, you know where any given score falls on that distribution. Sometimes, researchers convert all of their data to z-scores and then conduct analysis on those. I won't bother explaining why except to say that, occasionally, z-scores feed better into parametric statistical tests than do raw scores. By converting to z-scores, non-normal distributions sometimes change their properties so that they come closer to normality; this isn't cheating because the order of scores is still preserved. The highest scores are still the highest, and the lowest still the lowest and so on.

Sampling Distributions and the Standard Error of the Means

Finally, I can tell you something about the nature of *sampling distributions*, which is at the core of statistical testing. Whenever you sample data from a larger distribution, there is a chance that your sample doesn't really reflect the larger population. So, if I randomly select 10 apples from a bag of 100, there is a chance that the 10 I choose are bad apples, for example. Of course, if I keep on choosing sets of 10, and then average over the sets, I get closer and closer to describing the whole bag. The error within each set of 10 becomes diluted when I repeatedly select random sets of 10 and average across these samples. Another way of looking at this is by selecting a larger sample in the first place rather than subsequent small samples. Either way, you increase the chances that your sample *approximates to* the whole population (all of the apples in the bag). So, I can select two samples of 10 and then take the average over the samples, or I can select one sample of 20. The effect is largely the same. This is why, when psychologists conduct studies, they look to have large enough samples. However, they also look to replicate their findings by doing the same thing again on another set of participants.

OK, back to the numbers. When you sample from a set, and take the mean of that sample, you hope that it will be somewhere near the mean of the original set. If you take another sample, and another, and another, and another, and so on, you end up with a list of means for each sample. They will probably all be similar to each other, but they won't all be the same. Furthermore, none of them might be the same as the mean of the total set from which they all came. However, we assume that the mean of the means is the same as the mean of the overall population. We can then plot these means either side of the assumed population mean. We end up with a distribution of means, and we call this the *sampling distribution of means.*

Here's what I'm getting at. Imagine that we want to know how quickly the average 1-kW kettle boils. We take 100 kettles, and we fill them up, and select 10 randomly, and time how long each takes to boil. Then we put those back. We select 10 more, again randomly, then another 10, another 10, and so on, each time replacing the 10 we used before (which of course means that sometimes kettles reappear in the samples taken). So, we end up with the following times, in seconds: 58, 62, 55, 68, 66, 70, 74, 62, 59,

70. Each is the mean of the 10 kettles sampled. Now, the mean of these numbers is actually 64.4. As you'll see, none of the numbers is the same as that mean. Some are further away than others though. When you plot these as a distribution, you can then calculate the standard deviation of each of these means. You can judge each mean as a function of how far away from the overall mean (in our case 64.4) it is. In other words, you can use the standard deviation to tell you how much each mean is likely to be in error, a mistaken sample, if you like. However, when you calculate the standard deviation of a sampling distribution we have to call it something different, just to make it clear that it's a special form of standard deviation. We call it the *standard error*. Hopefully, you'll see why. The standard error is basically the average amount by which the sample means in the set differ from the overall mean, in other words the average amount of error contained in a sample compared with the scores it is chosen to represent.

The Central Limit Theorem

Finally, I can introduce the *central limit theorem*. You'll read about this, or hear about it, and might wonder what it is about. It certainly sounds grand and confusing, and if you're anything like me you'll panic slightly when you hear the word 'theorem'. Well, try not to. All that the central limit theorem says is that the more samples you take, the closer to the 'real' mean the average of those sample means becomes. In other words, the standard error reduces as you increase the number of samples that it is based upon. It's basically the idea that you dilute the error every time you add another sample mean to the mixture. Really, it's just common sense.

Now, as you know, in reality we don't tend to take hundreds of samples and then base our calculations on the average of all of them. What we do is select a large sample and hope that a single, large sample is enough. We use probability to estimate how likely that sample is to be erroneous. There is another way of judging how far off the mark our sample mean might be.

Confidence Intervals

In a way, when we say that the mean of our sample is X, we also should explain how confident we can be that the mean of the sample is somewhere near the mean of the population of scores as a whole. In fact, increasingly more psychologists report confidence intervals when they write research articles, and more and more journal editors are waking up to the importance of them. This is why I need to tell you something about confidence intervals here.

Think back to z-scores, and how they can be used to work out areas under a curve. Remember also that z-scores are similar to standard deviations, and that the standard error is a special kind of standard deviation. Therefore, z-scores, the standard deviation and the standard error are essentially cousins. They all tell you how far from the average a score is, and they can therefore tell you how much area under the distribution curve is cut off between your score and the mean of the set. So, in a real study we would have tested some people and ended up with a mean, or a set of means. How do I know that the mean is anywhere near the 'true' mean, i.e. that which I would achieve if I tested everyone on earth? The answer is that I can work this out using confidence intervals. Without boring you with the details of how these are worked out (because SPSS will calculate them for you), you end up with a sense of surety as to the mean of your sample representing the larger mean. Confidence intervals are based upon a percentage confidence (often set in advance at 95%). Ninety-five per cent is the standard because it reflects perfectly the 0.05 standard for alpha that we chose for most statistical testing. So, we can be 95% confident of what? Well, the 95% refers to how confident we are that the 'true' mean lies close to the mean we have sampled. So, we might report a mean of 12 with a 95% confidence interval of ± 2.44. What we mean is that we can be 95% sure that the 'true' mean lies within 2.44 units of 12. We could equally say that we are 95% confident that the 'true' mean (the population mean), is between 9.56 and 14.44. What I have done here is simply quoted the numbers that lie 2.44 either side of 12. As you might have now realised, a higher percentage figure combined with a smaller interval is the best scenario. For example, if we can be 99% confident that the population mean is almost exactly the same as our sample mean then we are in a strong position to claim that our study is, essentially, reliable, since our participants really are representing the human race. Conversely, if we are only 70% confident that the population mean lies within 10 units of either side of our sample mean of 25, we might as well have not bothered at all.

Σ SKEW AND KURTOSIS

When we collect data, and produce a frequency distribution of that data, perhaps also looking at the mean and standard deviation, we often find that it is not normally distributed. A very low standard deviation can tell us that the scores are tightly packed around the mean, and a high standard deviation can tell us that the data are widely spread around the mean. The former leads to a spiked distribution, called a leptokurtic one, and the latter a flat one (platykurtosis). I always remember these because the flat one is like a cross-section of the bill of a platypus, and leptokurtic distributions look like the middle has 'leapt up'. The problem a statistician faces is that most data don't quite fit a normal distribution, which might put them out of a job, since there are severe limits on what they can do with non-normal data. However, it's not quite so straightforward because we are not really faced with a 'yes' or 'no' decision about the normality of data. Most of the time, we have to consider the *extent* of normality (or, conversely, the extent of non-normality). It's more like a continuous scale, with some data being a lot more normal than others. Figure 2.3 shows two examples of varying degrees of kurtosis.

We can measure the extent of non-normality using two measures of the shape of the distribution. These are associated with the two ways that the shape of a distribution can actually vary. The peak in the middle can be high or low in comparison with the 'wings' or 'tails'. Also, the peak can be shifted away from the middle, creating a smaller tail at one end, and a larger one at the other. These two ways are called *kurtosis* and *skew*.

Kurtosis is concerned with the 'peakiness' or 'squashiness' of the distribution. Again, please remember that this is *in comparison with the tails*, since that's how we define these things. It's easier to *think* about the peak rather than the tails, but statistically the tails are what we are really assessing. The statistical program SPSS will compute a kurtosis statistic for you, and you need to be able to interpret it correctly. You should always check this before you proceed with inferential analysis, because a large degree of kurtosis can be a problem for you. A normal distribution is what we call mesokurtic, and the two extremes either side of this are platykurtosis and leptokurtosis. The figure that SPSS can give you will vary either side of zero. Zero kurtosis means that you have a normal distribution. Positive kurtosis values mean that the tails are very small in comparison with the

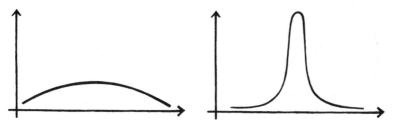

Figure 2.3 Platykurtosis (left) and leptokurtosis (right).

peak (leptokurtosis), and negative values indicate large wide tails and a low or non-existent peak (platykurtosis). When SPSS gives you a kurtosis statistic, simply compare it with the standard error next to it. If the statistic is more than twice the standard error, you should assume that the kurtosis is problematic enough to warrant a solution, which may be a transformation, or alternatively could involve selecting a non-parametric test instead.

Skew, as I have said, concerns the extent to which the peak is pushed off to one side, as if someone has sat on the one of the tails. Naturally, as the distribution can face one way or the other, we have positive and negative skew to describe this. When the tail is long on the right (peak over to the left) we have positive skew. When the tail is on the left with the peak shifted to the right, we call this negative skew (Figure 2.4).

When SPSS gives you skew statistics, positive numbers mean positive skew, and negative numbers indicate negative skew, as you'd expect. Again, you can guess that a skew of zero means that there is no skew at all. SPSS also gives you a standard error that is associated with the skew statistic. If the skew is more than twice the value of the standard error, assume the worst, i.e. that you have a problem with skew that needs to be addressed.

Therefore, in terms of statistics of skew and kurtosis, a normal distribution has values of zero for both. If you have a high level of skew,

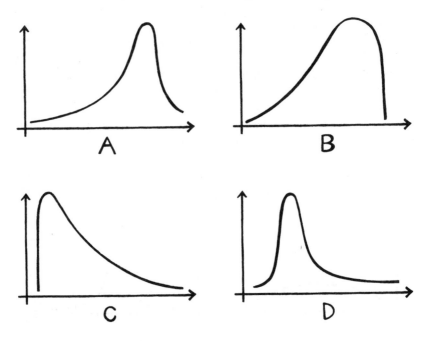

Figure 2.4 Examples of positive and negative skew.

this is generally seen as a worse situation than a high level of kurtosis, but it is safer to be conservative and consider both situations as challenges to your choice of statistical test.

Σ TRANSFORMATIONS

One of the useful statistical procedures that you'll almost definitely need at some point is transformation. What transformation involves is, basically, taking a set of data which does not meet our requirements, usually because it is non-normal, and converting it to something approximating normality by mathematically altering it, in some way, by performing some function. This is often achieved by taking the square root of each number, or by multiplying each number by a logarithmic constant.

So, we begin with non-normal data, and we alter them until they become normal. You might think that this sounds wrong. If the data are not what we would have hoped for, is it right to change them to transform their 'shape'? This is debatable. Some would say that all transformations are wrong, and that we should never attempt them. However, there is a world of difference between transforming data and outright cheating. When you transform data, you preserve some of their qualities. Furthermore, when you transform, you do it to all of your data, not some. So, what happens to scores in group A happens to scores in group B. In this sense, the treatment is equal. If I paint all the houses in my street, they look different. However, Olivia at number 5 still lives there, and I am still immediate neighbours with Clive on the left and Julie on the right. The people at the top of the hill remain at the top of the hill.

What won't work is simply multiplying all of your numbers, let's say by doubling each one. You cannot change the shape of a distribution by doing this. Try it if you like, as SPSS will easily allow you to do this. Halving them all won't work either, for exactly the same reasons. Square roots, however, do change distributions, because the square root of numbers is something much more special. To see how this works, just think about the fact that the square root of 4 is 2, whereas the square root of 9 is 3. The square root of 100 is 10. So, our original data could change from 4, 9, 100 to 2, 3, 10. The largest is still the largest, and the smallest is still the smallest, and the middle number still sits in the middle. However, we have cut off the massive tail by reducing that 100 right down to 10. Now, the largest number is five times the smallest, whereas before the largest number was 25 times greater than the smallest! You can see instantly how the shape of this set has changed. It has been 'transformed'. There are many transformations, and you'd need a good grasp of mathematics to understand what they actually do. However, you don't really need that level of expertise. What you do need to know is what kind of transformation is the best for what kind of data.

For a moderately positively skewed distribution, try the square root transformation. If the positive skew is stronger, then try a $\log_{10}$ transformation. When the skew is negative, you'll first need to reflect the scores. What this means is turning them all around so that the highest becomes the lowest, the lowest the highest, and so on. You can achieve this by looking at the highest score in the set, and adding 1 to that. Then take each number in the data away from this number. So if your numbers are 1, 3, 8, 12, 14, you add 1 to 14 to give you 15, then take them all from 15. You end up with 1, 3, 7, 12, 14. Then you perform a square root transformation. In the case of strong negative skew, reflect once more then apply a $\log_{10}$ transformation. SPSS will compute transformations for you provided that you tell it which one you want! Have you worked out why we reflect the scores for negatively skewed distributions yet? It's simple. By reflecting them, you turn them around, and they become positively skewed. That's how you can then apply the same transformations as you would with distributions which were positively skewed in the first place. Other, much more complicated transformations are possible, but it's probably not necessary to cover them all in this book.

One word of warning is important here. Transformations do not always work, so you should always check your data to see if the transformation you have applied has actually done the trick. So, always check for normality after a transformation. In addition, you must not mix transformations. Imagine a situation where you want to perform a correlation on variable P and variable Q, but where P is negatively skewed and Q is platykurtic. You would need different transformations for each to make them normal, but it isn't recommended that you do this. Instead, look to apply a non-parametric test.

3

PROBABILITY, POWER AND ERROR

The cornerstone of science is the testing of hypotheses. To the scientist, the only way that we can actually know if something is 'real' or not is to ask ourselves questions about it and then to seek the answers to those questions in a controlled, stepwise, methodical fashion, and to subject our findings to statistical rigour. That's the official story. The down-to-earth way of looking at this is that basically human beings are curious, and we like trial and error. In fact, even less intelligent species than ours can be observed wondering 'what happens when...'

Hypotheses work best when they are simple, and we cannot afford the luxury of intervening or confounding variables, which is why we have developed the specific way of testing hypotheses with as much control over the environment as possible. We keep everything constant, and try one thing at a time, so see what its effects are. Of course, it is possible to test multiple hypotheses at once using complicated designs, but each hypothesis is, in itself, a simple statement of the effect of X on Y. Experimental hypotheses are phrased in just this way. For example, increasing variable X will result in an increase in variable Y or there will be a positive relationship between P and Q. We sometimes call these alternate hypotheses. They are contrasted with a null hypotheses, which tell us about the state of affairs when X doesn't have an effect on Y, or P isn't related to Q.

Of course, statistics isn't about arrogance, or at least it shouldn't be. We cannot be 100% sure that anything we find is 'true'. That's the reason why we developed inferential statistical techniques. They allow us to *infer* that something *might* be true. How we go about inferring is based upon probability, which is why you need to understand probability to understand experimental science. You can't say that X does have an effect on Y, but you can say that it *probably* does, or very probably does, or almost certainly does.

I hypothesise that when I drop a ball it will fall to the ground. I set about testing this. I drop a ball, and it falls to the ground. Is that enough evidence? On its own, no. It might be a fluke. So I try it again, and again, and again. Slowly, I build up data that provide evidence that dropping balls makes them fall to the ground. After a thousand attempts, I stop. Can I be sure that I have now 'proved' this? Basically, I can't. All I can be sure of is that after a thousand trials, all have resulted in the predicted outcome. Of course, the very next one might prove me wrong. Or I might have to carry on to ten thousand, or a million, before I get my counterevidence. Even after a billion trials I can't be *sure* that dropping a ball *always* makes it fall to the ground. I would have to do it an infinite number of times to really be certain. However, the more times I test this out, the more my confidence grows. What statistical tests do is allow us to test an hypothesis and then attach a figure to that confidence. We call that figure a *P*-value, or probability value.

Let's imagine that I want to know if dogs live longer than cats. What I do is start taking records of dog and cat deaths, and I can then test my dog data against my cat data. I can't collect all the data that exist on cats and dogs, and I'm in a bit of a hurry, so I stop when I have 20 dogs and 20 cats. I can now calculate a mean age at which each species dies. Using a statistical test I can assess how different these two means actually are. In a way, I am looking at the separation of the peaks of two distributions of scores, assuming that they are normally distributed. I am making the important assumption that, somehow, my 40 animals represent all cats and dogs on earth. I conduct my statistical test, and end up with a probability of 0.05 that cats live longer. What does this actually mean? If we convert this to 5%, or 1 in 20, we can understand it better. It tells us that, although we have observed that cats live longer than dogs, there's only a 95% chance that this is 'real'. In other words, there is a 95% chance that the difference we have observed is actually the same as the one we would have observed if we had managed to collect data on all of the cats and dogs in the world. We have a *sample* of cats and dogs, not the whole population of them, which is why we can't have 100% certainty. Now, the observant amongst you might have noticed something very crucial about probability testing. The more participants in your study, the closer you get to the magic figure of *everyone*. If there are a trillion cats and dogs on earth, a study involving only one cat and one dog hardly makes a dent. However, the more you collect data from, the closer to that trillion you approach. Now, how close do you have to get for there to be enough? That depends on how confident

you want to be, which is why those *P*-values come into play. You don't
need to get anywhere near that trillion to be very confident indeed, because
large samples are *assumed* to closely mirror the population as a whole. This
is good for us, because we haven't got the time or energy to work with
entire populations. We *must* work with samples. Statistically, as our sample
size increases, it quickly reaches a point where we accept that collecting
more data won't make much difference. We still can't be sure that our
data are exactly the same as the data we would have if we found all of the
cats and dogs, but our *P*-value tells us how sure we can be, if all of our
assumptions about sampling are correct.

I keep using the word 'assumption', and there's a good reason for this.
Fundamental to all inferential statistics is the notion that samples *do*
represent the overall population. We can't be certain that they do, but we
hope that they do. On what does this hope rest? Here's the good bit... trial
and error. A long time ago, people tried this out by working out what
proportion of a population actually represents the whole population. You
can do this with numbers and calculating machines much more easily
than you can with real measurements taken from real people. If I make
up a distribution of scores, I can call that my population. I can plot these
using a frequency distribution to see what they look like. I can even put
these numbers on pieces of paper and put them in a bag. Then, I can
randomly pick 10 of them, and draw a new frequency distribution of just
those scores. What happens then is that I can compare that distribution
with my population distribution. It probably doesn't look much like the
population distribution. So, I put the 10 pieces of paper back into the bag,

SAMPLES
SHOULD REPRESENT
THE POPULATIONS
FROM WHICH THEY
ARE DRAWN...

and this time pick 20. I repeat the procedure, and, ever so slightly, the new frequency distribution looks more like the shape of the whole population. I try again with 30, 40, 50 and so on. Eventually, I pick enough numbers out of the bag that the distribution looks almost identical to the total, population, distribution. The curve is the same shape. Furthermore, if I put them all back in the bag, and pull out another set, *they* probably look almost identical to the population too. Can you see what I am achieving? I am able now to get a good sense of how representative different sizes of samples actually are. You should see now that this is why we aim for relatively large samples when we can. The bigger the sample, the more it is likely to represent the general population. However, at a certain point there's probably no reason to collect more data because the data we have is already representative *enough*.

The natural question for you to ask now is just how many that *enough* is... Well, actually, you'd be quite surprised at how little it is. The way the sampling distributions work, the difference between a sample and an entire population becomes infinitely small quite quickly. Infinitely small is the best you are going to get, if you recall, because the gap closes up completely only when the sample equals the population. You truly represent the population only when you *are* the population. There are various factors that affect the numbers involved, but a lot of the time you can represent a population of millions using a sample with only a few hundred scores in it. Just reflect on that for a second; it sounds wrong, doesn't it? Surely this is a mistake? How can 300 people be the same, to all intents and purposes, as a million? Well, so far I have missed something out. I haven't considered the assumption that the sample is actually properly selected. Three hundred people can represent 300 million people if you choose them carefully. There are actually two hidden assumptions in this issue of representativeness. The first, which most statistics textbooks tend to gloss over or completely forget, is that most 'things' have a lot in common. If you want a sample of people to represent a population of people, you inherently believe that people are very similar in lots of ways. If you want the weights of a set of rabbits to tell you something about the weights of all rabbits, you fundamentally feel that rabbits pretty much weigh the same, within certain limits. If you are going to use my CD collection to represent music taste of all people my age, you'd have to believe that all people of my age have very similar tastes. Now, see, it doesn't always work. But, most of the time, this whole process only hangs together because we believe that the property of a thing is shared by other things of that type. OK, now back to the assumption that everyone spends a lot of time talking about. This is the assumption of proper sampling.

If you look back to when I first started talking about sampling, I used the word *randomly*. That's also why I told you about plucking numbers from a bag. All of this rests upon a further assumption, which is that you have *randomly* sampled from the population when you collected your sample data. If you haven't, everything falls apart. Now I need to tell you what random sampling is. People have a tendency to talk about randomicity without really knowing what it means. These days, the word has crept into common usage. I often hear my students talking about 'some random guy' in a nightclub, or how they spent an afternoon looking around 'random' shops. However, this is technically incorrect. A genuine random sample is one in which every number (or person) has an exactly equal chance of being selected. The pieces of paper in the bag are just lying there and I could pick any of them. There are no favourites, and there is no *system* to my selection. Obviously, you'd have a very strange time bargain hunting if you genuinely wandered into shops randomly! If you made a choice not to bother with estate agents' premises, or pharmacies, or men's hat shops, then you have not been 'random shopping'. The moment you use selection criteria, you aren't really operating randomly at all.

So, let us recap. Testing a hypothesis allows us to generate data which may support that hypothesis. We can attach a figure to our finding which tells us how sure we can be that the finding represents what would happen if we tested everyone. The larger the sample, the more sure we can be. We usually don't need to work with absolutely massive samples because after a while a sample becomes so large that it is probably no different from

EVEN IF
BUSES
OPERATED ON A
RANDOM TIMETABLE,
SOMETIMES THREE
WOULD TURN UP AT
ONCE...

the entire population. However, strictly speaking this applies only if we randomly selected our sample.

Now, you might have spotted that we rarely use true random samples in research. This begs the question as to how we get away with it. If everything rests on random sampling, why isn't that what we always do? Why aren't non-random samples laughed out of the stadium? The answer is complicated, but I'll try to simplify it. The first consideration is that random sampling is not practical, and is often impossible. We have to make compromises, otherwise we'd all just go home. For example, there is the perennial problem of the fact that in psychology we only collect data from willing participants. Immediately, the sample isn't random. So, the best we can get is data from a sample of people randomly selected from willing participants. But, more problems then occur. Willing doesn't mean able. I can be willing to take part in your study, but if you can only collect data on Tuesdays because that's when the laboratory is free, and Tuesdays is a heavy teaching day for me, my willingness becomes irrelevant. So, your sample contains, at best, people randomly sampled from willing participants who were available. Now, if you happen to want to compare two age groups, 20–30 and 50–60, then random sampling from the wider population makes no sense. So, this time you end up trying to randomly sample from a population of willing volunteers who are available and meet the selection criteria. Somewhere, buried in all of this, is the intention to randomly sample, but there obstacles. In addition, true random sampling involves selecting from the whole population, assuming you have a list of them. When we start research projects we don't usually sit down with the telephone book and begin ringing up every tenth complete stranger listed.

The vast majority of student project research, and quite a lot of that conducted in other environments too, is based upon *opportunity samples*. We take who we can get, when we can get them, and very grateful we are too. We take the opportunity afforded to us by having other students around, or friends, or family, or colleagues, or whoever we can nab. Of course, they too have to be willing and able. So, why is this acceptable? Why can we do this? Well, some statisticians say it isn't acceptable. The trouble is, it's easy to say that this and that is out of the question, but that kind of negativity means that nothing would ever get done. Instead, most of us compromise, based upon another assumption. The assumption is that, most of the time, opportunity samples do not differ markedly from random samples. Therefore, an opportunity sample is assumed to have similar characteristics to a population sample. After all, if it holds true that most people are largely the same most of the time, it ought not to matter much that the person is available to take part and willing to take part. A lot rests on the idea that the people who don't want to take part are *not appreciably different* from those who do in respect of the variables being measured. We know that the unwilling and unavailable are different from the willing and available. But, that doesn't have to be a problem. If I am wanting to look at creative problem-solving, is there any reason to assume that the unwilling and unavailable solve problems quite differently from the willing and available? Of course there isn't. You'd have to work hard to think of reasons why that would be the case. Therefore, a truly random sample of people is unlikely to differ in the important ways from the opportunity sample we end up with.

Σ PROBABILITY AND *P*-VALUES

Before we get down to the important conceptual stuff, I need to clear up a few mathematical details. In my experience, many people seem to get tied up trying to understand decimal fractions. Probability is most commonly expressed in this way. Therefore, we see not only the standard cut-off point of 0.05, but also exact probabilities computed by modern software packages, such as 0.0034 and 0.67. I've seen people fill with dread when asked things about these. One of the greatest concerns I have is the number of students I have seen who cannot decide, at a glance, whether a particular *P*-value is greater or less than 0.05, which is something that every numerate psychologist must, without question, be able to do. Now, if you are one of those, don't worry. There's probably a good reason why you get confused, and there are lots of you out there. However, because there are many of you doesn't mean that it's OK. You *need* to know this. So, keep reading, please.

Mysterious numbers like 0.077 are simply there for you to compare them, in your head, against 1. In probability, 1 is the highest number. Zero is the lowest. *Everything* else falls between. So, we start at 0 and head off towards 1, and we need to work out how quickly we'll come across 0.077. In order to do this, if it doesn't just come to you naturally, you need to have a clear picture in your head of the various 'mileposts' on that journey. The main milepost is halfway, I reckon. Halfway between zero and one is 0.5. Every tenth of the way is 0.1, so we can divide into tenths thus: 0, 0.1, 0.2, 0.3, 0.4, 0.5, 0.6, 0.7, 0.8, 0.9, 1. So, 0.7 is bigger than 0.4, just as 7 is bigger than 4 or 7000 is bigger than 4000. Easy?

Now, each tenth can be further divided up into tenths, if you like. So, between 0.1 and 0.2 we have 0.11, 0.12, 0.13, 0.14, 0.15, 0.16, 0.17, 0.18

and 0.19. Again, 0.13 is bigger than 0.12, just as 13 is bigger than 12, or 13,000,000 is bigger than 12,000,000.

The thing about decimals is that you can keep on dividing them up. So, much as this is not nice on the eye (and a pain to type, I promise you), we can also divide the difference between 0.15 and 0.16 into yet more tenths. So, between 0.15 and 0.16 we have 0.151, 0.152, 0.153, 0.154, 0.155, 0.156, 0.157, 0.158 and 0.159. I hope you are still with me.

One more, and we'll stop, I promise. We can divide the difference between 0.154 and 0.155 too. So, between these we have 0.1541, 0.1542, 0.1543, 0.1544, 0.1545, 0.1546, 0.1547, 0.1548, and 0.1549.

I could actually spend the rest of my life typing divisions and subdivisions and sub-subdivisions and so on. In fact, the number of subdivisions is infinite. You can keep on adding decimal places. So, if someone asks you how many numbers there are between 0 and 1, the answer, depending on the definition of 'number', is that they are infinite. Similarly, there are infinite numbers between 0 and 10, or between 0 and 100. (If you really want to mangle your mind, ask yourself this; if there are infinite subdivisions between 0 and 1, or 1 and 2, or 2 and 3, there must surely be more than infinity between 0 and 10? And even more than that between 0 and 100, and so on. But infinity goes on forever, so can that be? Can you have more than infinity?)

Back to the job in hand. If decimal points worry you, you can actually forget about them when comparing the all-important 0.05 against any other figure. Here is how: whatever the number, look immediately after the decimal point. Is there a zero, or some other figure? If it is anything other than zero, the number must be greater than 0.05. If it *is* zero, what is the next number? If that next number is smaller than 5, then the number is less than 0.05. If it is greater than 5, the number is more than 0.05. There you go. No need to consider anything else. Of course, it is best of you truly grasp the idea of decimal numbers, but if you don't, this will help you to cheat.

Now I can get on with telling you about the basics of probability itself. All inferential statistics are based upon the notion of probability. We can never be certain of something, but we can express how close to certainty we can be. That's the first rule in statistics. This is why advertisements which talk about how some skin cream is *proven* to prevent wrinkles are technically incorrect. Proof means that we have 100% certainty, which in statistics (and in life, really) just can't happen.

All *P*-values that are churned out by statistical tests are an indication of the possibility that the null hypothesis is true, that is that whatever difference or relationship we have observed isn't really there. This is why

small *P*-values are a good thing. The smaller the *P*, the smaller the chance that our findings are erroneous, or flukes, or due to sampling error.

Now, the next step is a little more difficult to master. All statistical *P*-values are really what we call conditional probabilities. Something is conditional if it depends on something else being the case. For example, the following statements are conditionals:

- Given that I've got some eggs, we only need to buy ham to have ham and eggs.
- If I can get away early on Monday, we can go for a nice meal.
- Provided that it doesn't rain, we'll have a picnic.
- As long as I have the money, I'll go on holiday twice a year.
- If I can get 65% for my project, I should be able to manage a first overall.

So what has this got to do with statistics? Well, as you'll remember, I said that *P*-values are the chances of getting the result we have if the null hypothesis is the true state of affairs. That is, if the null is true, P represents the probability of obtaining the result that we have obtained from our data, or indeed a more extreme version of it. Therefore, P is conditional upon the null being true.

Let's imagine a box has six kittens in it. Some kittens are black, and some are white. I don't know how many of each there are, and I am only allowed to take out three kittens, without looking. Now, I am going to hypothesise that most of the kittens are black. Therefore, the null hypothesis is that there are precisely three black kittens and three white ones. I take out my three kittens, and they are all black. So, right now I know that at least three kittens are black. I can now make a probabilistic judgement about the chances of drawing out three black kittens *if* there are precisely three white and three black in the box. That is, I can work out how likely it is for me to draw three black kittens out if the null hypothesis is the true state of affairs. The actual way that the calculation works is not crucial for you, as long as you understand whatever the P-value I end up with means. However, logically, it works like this. If the null is true, the odds of the first kitten being black is 3 in 6, or 1 in 2. After the first kitten, there would be two black ones left and three white, so the odds of drawing a black kitten are now 2 in 5. The third black kitten has a 1 in 4 chance of being drawn. Remember that this is all assuming that there are three black and three white in the box. We multiply these together, and we end up with a P-value of 0.05. So, if there were an exactly equal number of black and white kittens in the box, the chances of drawing out three black kittens, one by one, is 5%, or 1 in 20. As you know, 0.05 is the cut-off point of choice for most statisticians, in that they tend to ignore anything greater or equal to that. Therefore, I cannot assume that most kittens are black just because the first three I pulled out were, even though there are only six in the box. There is an irony here. Have you spotted it? Statistically, I cannot be confident that most of the six are black having pulled out three. That's because the P-value is exactly 0.05. If it was slightly lower I could. However, I know there are six. If I were to pull out one more black kitten I wouldn't need a statistical test at all. I would now have four black kittens out of six, which of course *is* a majority. In fact, if you now work out the probability, you find that, if the null hypothesis is true, then another black kitten should not exist in the box, therefore of the three left the chances of drawing a black kitten out is 0 divided by 3. That gives you zero. Now, if you multiply 0.05 by zero, you get zero. This is really tidy isn't it? It mirrors common sense entirely. Now there is zero chance of ending up with four black kittens if there are only three in the box. We know that, of course, because we are logical creatures, but it's very comforting to see that the mathematics backs us up too! The calculation hasn't let us down. Tell that to the person who says you can lie with statistics!

Thankfully, we now have software which works out probabilities for us. Therefore, as long as you understand the way that probabilities relate to the null hypothesis then you can simply interpret the P-values that are handed to you, rather than have to figure them out for yourself with a lot of paper and a calculator (not to mention a pretty good knowledge of calculus to allow you to work out area under the curve...).

Finally then, let's paraphrase a P-value a few times so that this really goes in. Imagine I end up with a difference between A and B with a P of 0.01. Bear in mind that 0.01 is the same as 1%, or 1 in 100.

- There's a 1 in 100 chance that I would end up with an observed difference even if the difference isn't really there.
- There is a 1% chance that I would find this result (or a more extreme one) even when A and B do not differ in reality.
- Given a true null hypothesis, there is a 0.01 probability that I would detect a difference solely due to sampling error.

Just keep in mind that the null hypothesis refers to a whole population. We have merely sampled from a population when we conduct research. This is why this is all about the possibility of sampling error having occurred. It's also why we might speak of real and apparent differences. Your results are real, of course, but they are not real in the bigger sense of representing the whole population. A slice of cake is not the whole cake. Let's stick with cakes again for a moment. I tell you that I have baked a wonderful cake, and it certainly looks tasty. However, you are reminded of that terrible accident I had last time when I accidentally baked my watch into the cake. Now, there might be a watch in the cake this time, or there might not. So, it could be one big lovely cake, or a nice cake ruined by a watch somewhere in it. You really have to try some cake. It is tempting, regardless of my baking history. You assume and hope that there is no watch in the cake, and you have a slice. At this point, you can be sure that there is no watch only up to a point. You've had just a tenth of cake. No watch in a tenth. Now, you have another slice, and still no watch. So, by now you've eaten a fifth of cake and there is no watch. Does that mean the cake is watch free? Of course not. All you can say is that 20% of the cake is clear of watches! Only by eating the whole cake might you discover the true state of affairs. Probability is just like that. The only difference is that eating a whole cake is possible. There is no way that you can take all people on earth and get them to participate in your study.

Subjective Probability

There is a whole branch of psychology devoted to understanding subjective probability, and it's something that you can investigate elsewhere, but it is worth mentioning it here if only to point out that human beings are unreliable. Subjective probability is all about how people *perceive* likelihood, as opposed to mathematical probability, on which all inferential statistics are based. You might wonder why we actually need statistical tests at all. With the relatively small sample sizes on which most studies are based, you might argue that one can simply 'eyeball' the data and see what the trends are. The trouble with this is that people cannot be trusted. It's not that we are all liars, but rather that we cannot rely on the evidence of our senses and our interpretation of it. We are told that eating too many eggs is bad for our health, because they contain relatively high concentrations of cholesterol. However, some people instantly reject this because their own, personal, anecdotal evidence denies the fact. If you don't know a person who has suffered ill health because of eating too many eggs, and you eat lots of eggs yourself and are healthy, something seems wrong about the claim. Your *sample* tells you that eggs are fine. However, the claims are based on much bigger samples, and, more to the point, they come with a probability that says 'If eggs are not bad for you, then we would only get the result we have one thousandth of a per cent of the time. Thus, we conclude that eggs are bad for you in large numbers.' The egg-loving doubter has no way of determining how certain we should be of his evidence. Precisely because he relies on subjective probability in conjunction with a tiny sample his findings must be assumed to be very unrepresentative of the wider population.

Subjective probability isn't always such a terrible, misleading thing. Sometimes it is all we have. Have you ever wondered how we calculate the chances of life on another planet? Or how bookmakers are willing to let you place a bet on the chances of your son becoming a championship footballer who goes on to score a goal in the World Cup final in 25 years' time? We actually don't know for sure how many planets there are, and we don't know how many of them are likely to support life. Therefore, we make a guess. Similarly, the conditions for raising a footballer are very variable, and depend on thousands of factors, including natural talent, financial support, random factors such as injuries, and so on. Furthermore, even if your son becomes a championship footballer, he still needs to gain a place on the national team, be selected for the World Cup and be fit for it, and then whether he scores a goal depends on the rest of the team somewhat, and the other team, and the state of the pitch, and where the final is being held, including altitude and weather, which can affect fitness and ability to perform. We don't select World Cup host nations 25 years in advance, so this alone means that the calculation becomes largely impossible. (I haven't even mentioned the fact that only two teams make it to the final out of many more that participate...) Instead of even attempting to work this out, the bookmakers simply give you ridiculous odds, knowing that, although you might win, you probably won't. Therefore, the 10 pounds you bet might make you a multimillionaire in 25 years, but the bookmakers feel pretty confident that it won't.

Σ POWER

Now we turn to a set of related concepts: power, sample size and effect size. The whole purpose of conducting a statistical test is to detect some difference or relationship present in the data, assuming, of course, that it is actually present. Presence is rather important, because presence must exist in some amount. Something that is present has a certain size, weight and so on. Therefore, if you imagine that we are looking to pick up a difference between two groups of students on a mathematical task, the difference, if it exists, must be of a certain size. There must be a measurable amount of discrepancy between the two groups. We can conceptualise this in two ways, absolute or relative. An absolute difference is measured in terms of the actual scores obtained. Therefore, we might say that, on our mathematical test, which can yield scores of 0 to 50, the discrepancy between groups is of the order of three points on average. That's literally 3 out of 50. A relative difference can be specified in terms of percentage discrepancy, for instance one group scores on average 6% more than the other. Whichever way we do this, we are, effectively, specifying something called *effect size*. Just as we said that any relationship or difference in data that exists exists in some amount, so the amount is the effect size. If we expect or observe a large difference between two groups, thus we have a large effect size. A small difference is a small effect, and a moderate difference a moderate effect. The same applies for relationships between variables.

Statistically, effect size is all about separation between normal distributions of scores. (Well, it is for situations where we are looking for differences between means. In the case of relationships between scores, the strength of their relationship is the effect size.) Each group of scores has a distribution (hopefully a normal one). If we overlay these two distributions on one graph, we can compare the difference between their means. But what is even neater about this is that we can also look at the amount of overlap of the distributions. You can see this in the example in Figure 3.1. The greater the overlap between the distributions, the closer the means, and the smaller the effect. Less overlap equates to large effects. You can draw an exact mathematical relationship between measures of effect size (such as Cohen's d), and the percentage overlap between distributions.

Now, as you can imagine, the size of the effect will dictate the chances of finding it. A needle in a haystack is tricky to spot, even though it might be there. However, a pumpkin in a fishbowl is quite easily detectable. Now, as I said earlier, the function of statistical testing is to detect trends in data (differences and relationships). Big trends are easier to detect than small ones.

Now it gets more complicated. The real world is the real world; we can't necessarily tamper with that. So, if an effect is 'out there' to be detected, it is either small or large or medium-sized and there's nothing we can do about it. But if it's there, it's important not to miss it. It's analogy time again: somewhere in my carpet there's a staple. It fell out of a document. I can't leave it there, because it's sharp and someone might stand on it in their bare feet and receive an injury. I hope to find it, and I know what size it is: it's very small. I don't know where in the carpet it is. I get out my vacuum cleaner. The aim, of course, is to suck it out of tangled fibres of the carpet, and, because I don't know where it is, I have to simply sweep over the whole carpet (although I might miss a bit here and there due to human error... which means that I might miss the staple, in theory). What I

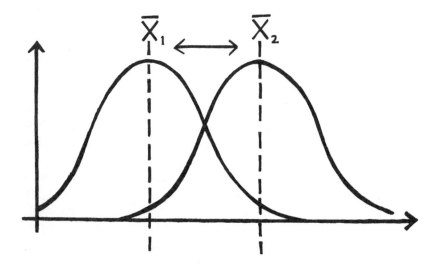

Figure 3.1 Effect size is related to the separation of the means of the sets of scores.

do know is that I have a vacuum cleaner with a certain power. What is the power of a vacuum cleaner? As you know, it relates to its ability to suck things up from the floor. Low power, weak vacuum, terrible chances of a good clean-up. High power, strong vacuum, clean floor! Now, if we take a trip back to statistical world, what do you think the *power* of a statistical test might be? Yes, like electrical appliances, tests are statistical appliances, and they too have power. The power of a test is a measure of its ability to detect a trend in data when it exists.

OK so far? Good, because the analogy is back, and there's more to learn. What if I told you that the staple can change size? Sorry, that's silly, but imagine that I don't know how big the staple is. Obviously, a bigger staple means that I probably have a much greater chance of sucking it up. The ratio of staple to carpet changes, and then so does my chances of finding it. The bigger the staple, the bigger the effect size. What about sample size? Any statistical test is carried out on data from a sample, and we tend to think that big samples are good. Now, this analogy only works on a fixed sample size. Effectively, the carpet is the sample from which we pluck the effect (the staple). In the real world of numbers and statistics, power, effect size and sample size work together in a particular way that doesn't quite fit the analogy. Two things can boost the power: increasing the sample size and increasing the effect size. We can't actually increase effect size because it is something that already exists. We can increase sample size, however. In our analogy, this would work as follows; we decide to vacuum the carpet more than once. The more times we sweep over it the greater the chance of sucking up the staple.

Now back to the statistics. What I'm trying to get across to you is the relationships that exist between these three factors: power, effect size and sample size. If you want to increase power, increase sample size. Or, you can decide to look only for large effects, and forget about smaller ones. The bigger the effect, the better the chance of finding it, obviously. Alternatively, you can increase sample size *and* look for larger effects, thus boosting power considerably. Most of the time you don't have any control over effect size, as I said earlier. So, moving the goalposts isn't acceptable. Therefore, the only way to increase power in most circumstances is to increase sample size.

Power is expressed as a percentage, or as a decimal proportion of the whole number 1. So, 0.9 and 90% are the same. This is just like the way that we express probability. That's because it is a very similar concept; in fact, power actually *is* a mathematical expression of probability. When power is 90%, it means that there is a 90% chance of success in sucking up the staple, if the staple is actually there (because in real life we don't know that the effect exists until we find it, of course). It's also essentially the same idea as that behind type II error. Type II error is the probability of keeping hold of a false null hypothesis, i.e. missing out on an effect because we assume that there isn't one there. Power is the chances of *not* doing that. Generally, we want power to be as high as possible. Note that just as *P*-values cannot reach zero, except theoretically, so power cannot reach 1.0 or 100%, except hypothetically. You can't say for certain that you *will*, undoubtedly, no question, find an effect if it is there. That's just too arrogant, basically. However, you can say you are pretty sure you will.

Prior to carrying out research, you can perform power calculations that allow you to set the sample size required in advance. Ideally, you want power to be as high as possible, but not so high that you'd need to recruit the whole world to take part in your study (which is what you'd need, incidentally, to achieve a power of 100%; can you see why that would be the case?). Most high-quality studies aim for a power of 80% (0.8) or above. OK, so we choose our power level, and then what? Well, power calculations allow us to deduce one item from three, that is we can work out the sample size needed only if we feed in the power and the effect size. Can you see the problem we now face? How can we possibly know the effect size? New research is all about finding out whether an effect exists, and if it does how big it is! So, we have three options. One is to base the effect size on what you know from existing research conducted on similar topics. You can only do this, of course, if that research exists. The next option is to decide what you regard as an important effect, in real life, and select that. This is a common option in medical studies, where, perhaps, you are specifically interested in cutting costs by 10%, or by making people 30% more satisfied with their care, or getting people back home after an operation 1 day earlier. Here there is a 'clinically significant' figure on which to base the calculation. However, our third option is the most likely for psychological studies. This is to be conservative without being too conservative. In essence, setting a large effect size as the target is silly unless you know it is large in advance (in which case why are you actually doing the research?). Setting a small effect size is equally silly, perhaps, since you make it difficult for yourself because of the massive sample sizes involved. Therefore, if in doubt it is probably best to select a medium effect size. You won't necessarily detect small effects, but you won't need to spend your life on the research either.

To give you a sense of the relationship between effect size and power and how they affect sample size, here is a rough example. Imagine a basic test such as an independent *t*-test, and let's decide to opt for high power around 90% and a small effect size (where the distributions of scores overlap by about 85%, i.e. the means are potentially very close together). In this case, you could end up with well over 1000 participants in your study. Reduce the effect size to a moderate one, and drop the power to 80%, and you are now looking at a study with, perhaps, only 200 participants. So, the moral of the tale is this: try not to set power lower than about 0.7 for smaller-scale student projects; be satisfied with detecting a medium to large effect and your sample sizes will be manageable.

Σ TYPE I AND TYPE II ERRORS

Every time we conduct a statistical test, there's a chance that our result is wrong. This is the case when we find a significant difference or relationship between scores, and also when we don't. If we end up concluding that there is a difference, for example, it does not mean that the difference is 'real', that is the difference might not hold up in the population as a whole. Similarly, when we conclude that there is no difference between means, it is possible that the true state of affairs is that there is a difference but we have failed to find it. This is what type I and type II errors are all about. No matter what we do, we will always have the possibility of one of them being committed.

Another way of understanding these errors is in terms of the hypotheses you generate to start with. If you start with the idea that A differs from B, and you find, in your study, that A differs from B, you might have committed a type I error, that is you might reject a null hypothesis when actually it is true. What we are saying here is that A and B are really just subsets of scores from a larger population, but we accidentally took some low As and some high Bs and then tested them against each other, which appears to show a difference between A and B. In actual fact, As and Bs should not differ because they are, in a sense, the same thing overall. So, if you tested all A scores against all B scores you would see that As are just Bs in disguise, or that A and B are just equivalent names used by C! Therefore, you rejected the null hypothesis but you are wrong to do so.

Alternatively, you can accept the null hypothesis and be wrong. Imagine that find that A and B scores do not differ. However, in the real world A *and* B scores are different. How can this happen? This time, you are pulling out A scores from a population, and you are pulling our B scores from a different population. However, the populations (or distributions) do overlap, and you happen to be sampling from the overlap area, not the non-overlap. This is shown in Figure 3.2.

So, if we tie our hypotheses up with the errors, we have effectively four states of affairs.

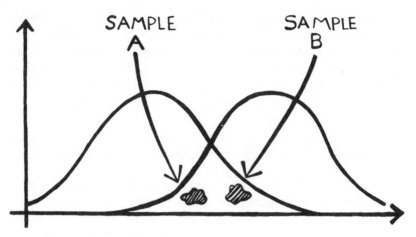

Figure 3.2 How type II error occurs.

- We think A and B differ, and in reality they do. No error.
- We think A and B do not differ, and in reality they do not. No error.
- We think A and B differ, but in reality they do not. Type I error.
- We think A and B do not differ, but in reality they do. Type II error.

As you can see, this means, in a sense, that we could be making an error half of the time. This is where the uncertainty of statistics comes in. It is not an exact science, because it involves making predictions about reality based upon little tests. So how do we get around these problems? Well, we cannot eradicate the possibility of these errors completely, but we can try to minimise them.

To reduce the possibility of a type I error we adjust the alpha level that we use to accept differences between A and B. Usually, we set alpha at 0.05. If we make it lower, say 0.01, we have to find a much more convincing difference between A and B before we accept it as 'real' or significant.

To reduce the possibility of a type II error, we can increase the number of scores in our sample. If something exists, it exists somewhere. If it exists somewhere, then the more places we look the greater the chance we will find it. If we have 1000 bags, and we only look for it in 10 bags, we could miss it. If we look in 900 bags, we will probably encounter it. If it isn't really there, then looking in 900 out of 1000 bags and failing to find it is a good indicator of its absence overall.

You might have noticed that we are always balancing out type I and type II errors, since trying to correct for a type I error can involve creating a type II error! If we say that we will accept only a result that is unlikely to occur by chance, we ignore all of the potential differences that are outside of that cut-off point.

An analogy might help here. I have a suspicion that Tina wakes up earlier than Bob. So, I rig them up to some equipment that detects what time each of them wakes up. However, I decide that a few minutes here and there are not enough to warrant a declaration that Tina is the earlier riser. Instead, I say that I am going to count only occasions when Tina wakes at least an hour earlier than Bob. Over a month of recordings, Tina never wakes up an hour or more earlier than Bob. I conclude that there is no difference between Tina and Bob. I accept the null hypothesis. However, a close inspection of the data shows that on most days Tina awoke earlier than Bob, on average 10 minutes earlier, varying from 1 minute to 39 minutes. Because I set my cut-off point at the wrong place, I didn't pick up on the difference that truly existed. I have committed a type II error, in essence.

Now, imagine that I decide to run a similar study with Bob and Frank. This time, I decide to look for any time difference, however small. In my timeframe of 1 month, on average Frank wakes up a minute earlier than Bob. I conclude that Frank rises earlier than Bob. However, if I were to have looked at this over a year instead of a month, I would have noticed that there is no difference between Frank and Bob at all. I simply chose an unusual month, let's say. In this case, the true state of affairs (no difference) was masked by a temporary difference, which boils down to an error in my sampling. Now I have committed a type I error, by assuming a difference where there isn't one. This can occur when I set the cut-off point too low. If I will accept any difference as a real one, then a fraction of a second difference between Tina and Bob could lead me to assume that this is a real, and meaningful, separation. However, very small differences might not be meaningful, and could be the result of a problem occurring with the measurement system, for example. I might use two identical clocks or stopwatches to measure waking up times, but for some reason one of them is ever so slightly out of kilter with the other in a systematic way. It therefore seems that they get up at different times when they truly don't. By only choosing to accept differences greater than a certain amount we reduce this kind of error.

What you should have noticed here is not just the interplay between type I and type II errors, but also how these are affected by alpha and by sample sizes, and by the magnitude of the difference being looked for. Essentially, the ideal state of affairs for reducing all errors is this: the difference we are looking for is big, and the sample size is big. In such cases, we can say that our chances of picking up the difference is also large. We refer to this as

our power, and we should always aim to have high power. When power is low, we can easily fail to detect a difference that is genuinely there.

One more thing to remember here: I have chosen to use the term 'difference' throughout this book because I didn't want to confuse you. However, tests don't only pick up differences. Sometimes we are looking for relationships between variables, as in correlation. The same issues apply in correlation, even though the tests we used to detect relationships are not the same ones as for differences.

4

FIRST STEPS IN INFERENTIAL TESTING

Σ   t-TESTS

There are a number of forms of the t-test, and it is important that you know the differences between them, and that you understand the underlying principles of the notion of t-testing. Even students who are familiar with conducting and applying t-tests often cannot explain what t itself actually is. Here I hope to answer that question and to leave you with no doubt which t-test is which.

Most textbooks on statistics begin the section on t-tests by telling you about the man who invented the test, and how he worked for a brewery and so on. I'm deliberately going to avoid all of that, because I'd like you to read about it elsewhere if you are interested. I'll stick to the things you really need to know.

There are two main forms of the t-test, and they correspond to the two main forms of design possible when you are looking at comparing two groups of scores. In one scenario, the scores are derived from different people. In another, they are derived from one group of people who are tested twice, perhaps at different points in time, or on slightly different versions of some task. The first of these scenarios, as you will know, involves a between-groups design, and the other is a within-groups design. When we have a between-groups design, the *independent* t can be employed, whereas a within-groups design necessitates the use of what we call the *related* t.

So, we'll cover the independent t first, because once you've grasped that the other one follows nicely. Essentially, the independent t-test compares the means of two groups of scores derived from different sets of people, and tells you if they are significantly different from each other. Another way of looking at this, which is technically more accurate, is that the test tells you about the chance that those two means have come from two identical populations of scores. There are two ways that two sets of numbers can differ. In the first case the numbers are different because the populations are genuinely different, and in the other they are different only because you pulled them out of two different ends of one larger set. This can be seen in Figure 4.1.

So, when you end up with a significant difference, you are being told that, although we can't be totally sure that the scores aren't two ends of a larger set, it's unlikely that they are. This is important because it is where the all-important '*t*' comes from. *t* is a distribution, just like a normal distribution. It is simply an adjusted version of the normal distribution that works better for smaller samples. For sample sizes greater than about 30 it effectively *is* the normal distribution. It is, if you like, a way of expressing a ratio of between-groups variance to within-groups variance. For a test of between-groups difference, the gap between one mean and the other should be bigger than the variance found within each group. So, we look at the difference between group A and group B and we compare that with the differences found between scores within each group (highest to lowest etc.). The logic is that meaningful differences will show up in the gap between A and B, and non-meaningful differences are found within the groups. If there are more meaningful differences than non-meaningful ones, then *t* will be higher. Higher *t* equates directly to significant differences. Therefore, when you have looked at lots of results from *t*-tests you will notice that when *t* is higher, *P* is lower. A high *t* tells you that the difference between means is large. Not only that, but that it is so large that it is unlikely to have occurred due to chance, or, more correctly, due to sampling error. So, lower *P* means that such a difference is unlikely (but still always possible)

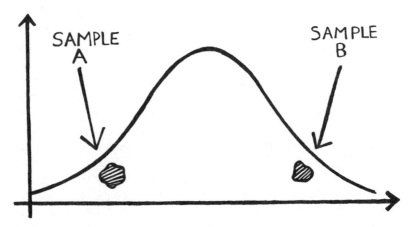

Figure 4.1 Samples drawn from extremes of a single population.

to have occurred because you drew your samples from different ends of one bigger set of scores. In fact, if you understand this, you understand most of what inferential statistics are about.

The related t-test works on very similar principles but is used when the scores you have come from one group of people tested more than once. We need a different test for just one reason really. It's all to do with variance. Furthermore, this explains the word 'related' too. It sounds very odd, I know, but how related am I to you? You might be tempted to say 'not at all'. However, that isn't true. We are all related to some degree, however tiny. But, that degree of relatedness is so small that we can ignore it. You and I probably share some genes which go back thousands and thousands of years to some common ancestor who we cannot possibly trace back. So, you and I are pretty much independent of each other. That's the logic behind the independent t-test: two groups of people, unrelated. In fact, the independent t is sometimes also called the unrelated t. However, the related t is used when one group of people is tested more than once. This time, the groups of scores are regarded as highly related to each other because they come from the same source. It's a very odd question, but how related to yourself are you? The answer is that you are just about as related to yourself as it is possible to be. One hundred per cent really. Now, to be

BOB GETS HIS t-TEST HORRIBLY WRONG

specific, how related are two scores that come from you? Again, they must be quite related because of the common source. Therefore, we can regard scores coming from one set of people as being related, because they will have a lot of common variance behind them. This is why the related *t* exists. When we compare between-groups variance to within-groups variance, the nature of that ratio will differ depending on how much shared variance we can actually expect. The related *t* accounts for the additional relatedness we can expect in the scores we have obtained. Again, we end up with a value of *t*, and again this is reflected in the *P* value that comes with it. The related *t* is basically an independent *t* with a correction to account for the correlation between scores that you expect to happen when they come from the same people.

There is another form of the *t*-test that you should know about, called the *one-sample t*. I think I have used it about three times ever, but each time I was very glad that I knew about it and had that tool available to me. Just as it sounds, the one-sample *t* is a form of the *t*-test that allows you to compare the mean of a sample you have obtained with another mean that already exists. That's why this is a special form of the *t*-test that is rarely used. You need to know the mean of another sample already. Otherwise, this is a fairly straightforward version of the *t*-test, and is easily calculated using statistical software. You might have used SPSS many times without even noticing that it can calculate one-sample *t* tests for you. So, why do we sometimes already know the mean of one of our groups, you might wonder? One circumstance could be where we have norms of a particular test already established. For example, we know what the average score on an IQ test is. By definition, it is 100. Therefore, if we want to know whether a particular group of people are more or less intelligent than average, we only need test one group, our population under question. We then take their scores and test then against that average of 100, which is often referred to as a 'user-defined mean'. The one-sample *t*-test then compares the scores we have obtained against 100, and tells us if they are statistically different from each other. Another way of using this test, perhaps more controversially for some statisticians, would be where you want to decide whether a group of scores differs from some arbitrary cut-off point that we have decided upon. For example, you might decide (in advance of your data collection) that you will only take seriously a particular range of scores you observe. So, if you have a test of perceived stress with scores that could range from 0 to 20, you might decide that you will regard as unimportant a mean stress per group of less than 15. So, effectively, you are saying that 15 is your cut-off point, and you are hypothesising, in advance, that your participants will score more than 15 on the test, because you are predicting high levels of stress in that population. Now you can go ahead and test your population, and then set your user-defined mean at 15. The one-sample t then compares your observed scores with your criterion, and tells you if your scores are significantly different from the benchmark number you set.

When Significant Differences Aren't What You Need

There is just one more use of t-tests that you should be aware of. It's perfectly legitimate but not often used. It is perhaps, I suspect, because it involves a little 'thinking outside of the box', which not everyone is willing to do with statistics!

Ideally, when we want to conduct an experiment in which we manipulate just one independent variable and hold everything else constant, we ensure this constancy by matching our groups. So, we make sure that our two groups do not differ in age, or ratio of men to women, or any number of other variables that we might think could have an effect on the outcome if we are not careful. Of course, in the real world we can't always do this kind of matching. A lot of the time we must make do with opportunity sampling, taking our participants, of whatever type, wherever we can access them. We can't always be choosy and dictate what age or sex we want them to be. However, let us take an example of a scenario in which we have two groups, tested on vocabulary. One is a group of librarians and the other is a group of sales assistants. Our hypothesis is that the librarians will score significantly higher on the vocabulary test than will the sales assistants. The logic is that librarians, spending a lot of time with books (and therefore words), will have better vocabularies. So, we went to a library and tested librarians, and we went to a shop and tested sales assistants. We did not have the luxury of controlling for other variables. We were grateful for the participants we got, when and where we got them. However, we are aware that as we age our vocabularies tend to increase. Therefore, age is potentially a confounding factor that we wouldn't want contaminating our findings. We couldn't match our two groups on age in advance, but it might mess things up if we found that our librarians were older than our sales assistants or vice versa. We wouldn't know whether their jobs or their ages were contributing to any effect we observed. So, what we can do is test the two groups against each other using age as a 'temporary' dependent variable. We conduct an independent groups t-test comparing the ages of the librarians with the ages of the sales assistants. Now, this is the odd bit. We are conducting this test precisely because we do *not* want to see a statistically significant difference emerging. We wish to be able to report that the groups did not differ in age. Therefore, when we perform our all-important t-test to compare sales assistants with librarians on vocabulary scores, we can be sure that our result is not contaminated because one group happens to be older than the other.

Σ LEVENE'S TEST

One of the important assumptions that parametric difference tests make is that the means being compared come from data with equal variances. We might want the means to be different, but not the variances, because then we are not comparing like with like. This is the assumption of homogeneity of variance. If the variances are unequal, problems can occur. We can simply look at the variances and see if they seem similar, but we are faced with not really knowing how similar is similar *enough*. Luckily, there is a statistical test which does this for us, saving us from the difficulty. This test is called Levene's test, and SPSS will compute this as a matter of course. The beauty of this test is that we can see whether the variances of the groups being compared are significantly different from each other. Levene's test is automatically computed by SPSS when you have run an independent t-test. In fact, homogeneity of variance is really an important criterion only when you have an unrelated or independent t on your hands, and when the sample sizes of the two groups are markedly different. This is because the unrelated t-test formula deals with variance in a particular way. It is pooled across the two groups, which basically means that it is averaged. Why? Well, the null hypothesis assumes that the two sets of data are drawn from very similar or identical populations of scores. This would mean that they would be similar in variance. As the samples are meant to represent the whole, then two samples would represent the whole better than one. Therefore, we count them together. You cannot do this, of course, if they are very different, since pooling them achieves nothing. Therefore, in this case you should always check the result of the Levene's test very carefully. Here's where many students get confused. What you want to see is a non-significant Levene's. This is difficult to remember at first, because you are taught to look for significant differences and significant relationships, and so seeing something less than 0.05 seems like a good thing. However, in the case of Levene's, you *want* >0.05! No significant difference in a Levene's means that the variances of the two groups under test are not different from each other. That is, you have homogeneity of variance. Remember it like this:

- Levene's is a test of difference.
- Levene's tests variances to see if they are different.
- We want homogeneity of variance in our data.
- The 'homo' bit means 'same'.
- Significant Levene's means different variances, so that's bad.
- Non-significant Levene's means equal variances, which is good.

When SPSS gives you a line in the output for 'equal variances not assumed', which, as I have said, you look at when Levene's test is significant, that line is actually Welch's t, even though it isn't labelled as such. So, when someone refers to Welch's t, they are referring to the correction for heterogeneity of variance.

ANALYSIS OF VARIANCE

Σ ANALYSIS OF VARIANCE (ANOVA)

There's a reason why this is called analysis of variance. Unlike other tests, which are often named after people, such as the Shapiro–Wilk, this one actually tells you what it does. It analyses variance. You are advised to read the section of this book on *variance* and the section on *t-tests*, and then come back here. Variance is like love. It comes in two forms: the kind you want and the kind you don't want. Analysis of variance compares the kind you want with the kind you don't want, and if you have more of the kind you want you're in luck. To be specific, you usually want *four times more*. When the wanted variance is four or more times greater than the unwanted, you generally have a statistically significant effect. This ratio of one kind of variance over the other is called the *F*-ratio. Look in your textbooks and statistics outputs, and you'll find it there. I'll come back to it later.

So, what do we mean by variance we want and variance we don't? Well, we mean that there is effect variance and error variance. We want the effect variance. I know you're still puzzled, but you won't be soon. Just bear in mind that the word 'error' means something specific to a statistician. It doesn't mean 'mistake'. It means 'unwanted'. Error variance is also occasionally called noise. In this situation, noise isn't a sound! To a statistician, noise is something going on in the numbers that interferes with what you want to see.

Two sets of numbers can *vary* in two ways. They can vary inside themselves, or between each other. In ANOVA, we are looking for the sets to vary more between each other than they do inside themselves. So, if we take some examples: 9, 9, 9, 9, 9, 9, 9 and 2, 2, 2, 2, 2, 2, 2 are two sets of numbers. How much do they vary inside themselves? Well, all the 9s are 9s, which means that the variance is non-existent, and the same applies to the 2s. But when you compare the sets, you see that every number in one set is different from every number in the other set. Another way to look at this is in terms of distances between numbers.

9 is 0 distant from 9, and so on.
2 is 0 distant from 2, and so on.
9 is 7 distant from 2, and so on.

We then add up the distances from each source and compare them. Therefore, the total variance in the 9s is 0, and the total variance in the 2s is 0. This gives us no variance at all in the 'insides' of the sets. What about between? As you can see, we have seven 7s. Any fool can tell you that 49 is bigger than nothing. That's effectively what ANOVA is doing. Of course, I have deliberately chosen really simple, extreme examples. It's harder for you to get the point with real, likely, data. (I am also missing out some fine details here, but as long as you get the idea, you can read about the true calculations in any other statistics book.)

What if I told you that the 9s and 2s were the numbers of words remembered by participants in two groups of an experiment? One group was tested in the middle of the day, the others were woken up in the middle of the night and tested straight away. So, as you would expect, we are looking to see if memory is better when you are fully awake. Let's imagine the 9s are the daytime scores and the 2s are the night-time scores. We are hoping to find an *effect* of time of day. The *effect variance* is essentially the differences between the means in the two groups. We usually call this the 'between-groups variance'. We compare this with the variance *within* the groups (essentially an error variance, since we don't want it). This is the 0 that we worked out. In this particular case, the result is obvious. As I mentioned earlier, the *F*-ratio is a statistic that shows you how much bigger the between-groups variance is than the within-groups variance. We would be able to conclude, in our example, that people remember words better when you test them in the middle of the day than when you test then after waking them up in the night.

So, it's analogy time. What ANOVA does is look for a needle in a haystack. The between-groups variance (effect variance) is the needle, and the error variance (within-groups variance) is the haystack. Now, it's not easy to look for a needle in a haystack. However, that really depends on the relative sizes of the needle and the haystack. A massive needle in a tiny haystack is fine by me; the other way around, less so.

Now we can deal with the more complicated uses of ANOVA. Up until now, we've dealt with only two groups, but ANOVA is intended for more than that. It allows you to compare sets of scores (and their means) when you have quite a lot of them. You might ask why we don't just use *t*-tests. Well, you may be surprised to learn that ANOVA is very similar to running multiple *t*-tests to look for differences between lots of groups, but it does so in a special way that avoids a big problem, which is the fact that when you run multiple tests you increase the chances of messing them up. (This is explained where we deal with *type I error, type II error* and *familywise error*.) ANOVA *protects* against this problem. Protection is not just a nice way of describing this: it is the proper statistical term.

The simplest ANOVA is the one-way. You would normally do this with three or more groups. So, if we stick with my memory example, I am now collecting scores from people tested at 3 am, another group tested at 11 am, and another at 5 pm: three groups. This time, I'll use some slightly more realistic scores. Look at Table 5.1.

Hopefully, you can see what's going on here, even though the numbers are a little less tidy than in the previous (two-group) example. Can you imagine what a one-way ANOVA does with these scores? It works out the within-groups variance and compares it with the between-groups variance.

This comparison of the scores from three groups is achieved using a one-way ANOVA. It is called this because there is only one path through the numbers that you are interested in; it is the path across the three groups. You are looking for differences between those groups, and comparing them with the error variance found within the groups. In theory, you can have as many groups as you like in a one-way ANOVA. However, you should be aware that the ANOVA will find differences, but won't necessarily tell you where they are. If you conduct a one-way ANOVA across the three groups in the above example, you may well find a significant effect of time of day (as we would refer to it). Now, what does that mean? It means that at least one of the three groups has different scores from at least one other. It

Table 5.1 Some data for a one-way ANOVA.

3 am	11 am	5 pm
2	8	9
1	9	8
3	7	8
4	6	8
2	9	8
2	9	8
3	7	9

doesn't mean that all of the differences are significant! We have a number of potential differences:

3 am and 11 am
3 am and 5 pm
11 am and 5 pm

Your ANOVA may pick out a significant effect of time of day even if only *one* of these comparisons is actually significant. You will need further tests to discover which differences are significant and which are not. These tests will allow you to pick out individual groups and compare them with each other, in exactly the same way that you might conduct *t*-tests between

S TATISTICAL TESTING NOW A
CRIMINAL OFFENCE. USE OF
ANOVA LEADS TO OVERCROWDING
IN PRISONS.

pairs of scores. These are covered in more detail in the sections dealing with *planned comparisons* and *post hoc* tests.

Now, we can consider *two-way* ANOVA, and other such tests. Sometimes we are interested in the effects on a dependent variable of more than one independent variable. Instead of just time of day, we might be interested in the age of the participants. We could just run two separate one-way ANOVAs to look for the separate effects of each independent variable on the dependent variable. However, that is a bad idea for three reasons. Firstly, you should never run multiple tests when one test will do. The more tests you run, the greater the chance of error (see the sections on *type I error, type II error* and *familywise error*). Secondly, because ANOVA is analysis of *variance* it helps if you have all of your variance in one analysis! Basically, every person has an underlying level of variance that they can contribute to just about anything you might measure. Call it their 'personal variance' if you like. It is effectively common to everything that they do. Let us take an example of a person who is tested at 3 am and is 'younger'. When that person is contributing variance to a group that they are in, let us say the '3 am' group, they are also contributing variance to the 'younger' group too. If you analyse the effects of time of day and age in two different analyses, the common variance cannot be taken into account. Put all the variables into one analysis and it can. The third reason why you should not separate out analyses when they could be put together is that you really want to look at your factors *in relation to each other*. You want to know if the pattern of scores observed across time-of-day groups is different depending on whether you are looking at younger or older participants. Or, you want to know if the difference between younger and older participants' memory scores is preserved across separate times of day. (You might have noticed how much these statements are starting to feel a little like hypotheses.) What I am getting at is *interactions.* ANOVA with multiple factors allows you to investigate the interactions between those factors. Quite commonly, the most important hypotheses in research are those concerned with interactions between variables. I'll come back to interactions shortly.

In the example we have used already, let us consider that we also want to look at the effects of age on this memory test. We know that older people differ from younger people in their ability to remember things, so let's throw in age as another factor in the ANOVA, this time with two levels. So, now we have three time-of-day groups and two age groups (for the sake of argument, we could just call them 'younger' and 'older'). We can describe the analysis we would do as a 3×2 between-groups ANOVA. First of all, you will notice that we need a table of descriptive statistics (means and standard deviations) that contains more information than we have for a simple one-way ANOVA. We now have *six* cells in our design; these are 3 am younger, 11 am younger, 5 pm younger, 3 am older, 11 am older and 5 pm older. Table 5.2 shows the results of our research efforts in a table of descriptive statistics.

Look very carefully at Table 5.2 and take note of the 'marginal means', as we call them (sometimes we refer to them as 'collapsed means'). Not only can we see how each of the six groups of people have scored (along with the spread of those scores through the standard deviation), we can also see how each of the factors works independently. That's what the marginal means show. Therefore, we can see the effects of age (younger versus older) whilst blissfully ignoring the effects of time of day. Alternatively, we can forget all about age, and simply look at the three time-of-day groups. The data, when fed into an analysis of variance, end up being grouped just like this, but the ANOVA also allows us to look at the interaction between the two factors. Therefore, an ANOVA performed on these data will yield three *terms* (which is the proper technical word we use). Two are what we call 'main effects', and the other is the 'interaction term'. You will note that the younger people seem to remember more than the older ones. The ANOVA tells us that there is a main effect of age. What the test does, as you will probably have worked out from the earlier description of the workings of ANOVA, is compare the variance between the data from the two age groups with the variance within those groups. We can also see that there is a main

Table 5.2 Means and marginal means for a 3×2 design.

Age	Time	Mean	SD	N
Younger	3 am	3.40	1.14	5
	11 am	5.40	1.14	5
	5 pm	7.20	0.84	5
	Total	5.33	1.88	15
Older	3 am	2.00	0.71	5
	11 am	3.20	1.64	5
	5 pm	4.60	0.89	5
	Total	3.27	1.53	15
Total	3 am	2.70	1.16	10
	11 am	4.30	1.77	10
	5 pm	5.90	1.60	10
	Total	4.30	1.99	30

effect of time of day. Again, the ANOVA compares between-groups variance with within-groups variance. Finally, the ANOVA describes the interaction between those two factors in statistical terms. It compares the patterns of younger and older participants' scores when you take time of day into account. In other words, it asks whether the better performance of younger people is similarly better no matter what time of day it is. Conversely, it looks to see if the difference in performance for the three times of day is the same no matter how old the participants are. A significant interaction means that there is a discrepancy somewhere in the pattern. This can be due to just one group out of the six being out of line. Of course, it can be due to more than that.

We can look at the two main effects and the interaction by analogy. The data are a cake. Not just any cake, but a magic cake. When we cut it, and then shove the slices back together, it joins up into a whole cake again. First, we cut the cake to give us two pieces. Each piece represents the scores from the younger or older age group. If the pieces are different sizes, we have a main effect of age.

Now, we put the pieces back together, and wait a little for the magic to work. *Voilà*: a whole cake again. Then we cut it into three pieces. This time each piece represents the scores from the three time-of-day groups. We can see that they are not the same size. We have a main effect of time of day.

We can now make a second cut. We leave the three pieces, but we cut them in the other direction to split each piece into two, preserving the relationship between younger and older groups. That is, the younger piece is going to be bigger. We end up with six pieces. If at least one piece is bigger (or smaller) than at least one other, we could have an interaction on our hands. It's a bit more fiddly than this, but I hope you get the idea.

If this is still proving a little difficult for you to imagine, we can try another analogy, this time for a 2×2 ANOVA. Imagine I have a set of balls,

some of which are red and some blue. Colour is, therefore, a variable. But what if some balls are striped and some have spots? Now we have a second variable, pattern. If I ask you to divide the balls into two sets based upon a criterion that you choose, you could pick *either* pattern or colour. Each set that you create still contains elements of the other variable, however. If you divide them on the basis of colour, then a proportion of the red balls will be spotted and a proportion will be striped. Just because you are focusing on one variable doesn't mean that the other isn't there. When you look at a friend, you don't see molecules. They are there, but you don't see them. If you had microscopic eyes that allowed you to see the molecules, you still wouldn't see a buzzing mass of quanta of atomic energy, even though that's there too, 'underneath' the molecules. Back to the balls. If I want to look for differences in colour, I could count the number of balls that are in the red set and the number in the blue set. If they differ, I could, if I were doing this with proper statistical tests, say I had a main effect of colour. Similarly, I could temporarily ignore colour and look for a main effect of

pattern. Again, I would be able to look for a difference in the number of striped and the number of spotted balls. That leaves just one question, or some inter-related questions:

Is the proportion of striped to spotted balls the same or different for each colour?
Is the proportion of blue to red balls the same or different for each pattern?

This time, we need to separate out the balls into four sets, which are blue and striped, blue and spotted, red and striped and red and spotted. Now we can count them. Does each set contain a quarter of the whole? Maybe, maybe not. Is one set much smaller or larger than all of the others? Now we've reached the end of this analogy, because right at this moment we are considering what an interaction in a 2×2 ANOVA might be about. Hopefully, you've got it. Variables can be called all sorts of fancy things, and long variable names can load up your working memory, so that instead of being able to get to the root of the analysis, you confuse yourself trying to remember what's what. If it helps, conceptualise every 2×2 that you come across as a set of balls, some blue, some red, some striped, some spotted. Then, at the end, when you've understood what is happening, stick the original variable names back on.

Another way of looking at interactions is in terms of parallel lines. If you plot mean scores for all six groups on a graph, and then join the dots across the points which represent a variable you can ask yourself if the lines in front of you are parallel, or following a similar shape, or if they are very different, perhaps even crossing over.

Now, we have just used two between-groups factors so far, but if you imagine a study with five factors, you can then start to reflect on what can happen when you try to understand the nature of any interactions that the ANOVA picks out. For example, imagine if we have five factors with two levels of each. For example, these might be age (younger/older), sex (male/female), IQ (low/high), smoking status (smoker/non-smoker) and educational status (lower/higher). What would you do if you ended up with an age × sex × IQ × smoking status × educational status interaction? What would that mean? Could you make sense of it? I know I couldn't. What is more, it's also impossible to plot this graphically, so you can't even make it clearer by drawing a picture! ANOVA is a great tool for understanding how variables work together to lead to certain effects, but it is limited. When people say that you can do just about anything with statistics, they are really quite wrong.

Repeated Measures ANOVA

Apart from the way that variance is calculated and shared across groups, ANOVA using repeated measures factors is the same as a between-groups ANOVA. Just as the between-groups ANOVA is like a bunch of unrelated *t*-tests stuck together, so the repeated measures ANOVA can be conceptualised as a collection of related *t*-tests tied up in one calculation.

Mixed ANOVA

Sometimes known as split-plot ANOVA, this type of analysis of variance is used when you have a mixture of between-groups variables and within-groups variables. For example, I might be interested in looking at people's memory of two types of events (let's say one boring and one interesting), and how this is affected by their personality (broadly divided into introvert and extrovert) and by their education (university or non-university). In this example I would have two between-groups independent variables and one within-groups independent variable. There is one dependent variable, that is their memory score. Now, when you compute this in SPSS, you end up with ANOVA tables which you must not get mixed up over. The effect of the repeated measure (within-groups variable) will be found in the table that shows repeated measures and the effects of the between-groups independent variables will be found in the between-groups effects table. The interactions will be easy to find because they will be listed with '*' between them, which substitutes for 'x'. You need not concern yourself in the detail of how these have been calculated at all. The output is just as easy to understand as when you are looking at a simple independent variable with just one type of variable (*either* between or repeated). The reason for using mixed ANOVA is simply that you can tuck all of the effects into one analysis, thus reducing error and saving time.

MANOVA

So far we have been dealing only with situations in which there is only one dependent variable, i.e. one measurement that we are looking for changes in depending on other factors. However, ANOVA will allow you to look at multiple dependent variables, and that's what MANOVA is. It stands for 'multivariate analysis of variance' (also known as multiple analysis of variance)! If you didn't perform MANOVA, you would have to run separate

ANOVAs for each dependent variable. By now, you might be able to guess why this is not a good idea. It's the same issue that rears its ugly head whenever you conduct sets of tests separately, that of familywise error. Multiple tests mean that you are having more than one attempt to find a significant difference across groups, which in itself is not so bad, but when you have set the same alpha level for each test (usually 0.05 of course), you end up compromising that alpha by sharing it across the set of tests. What you are doing is saying 'I'm going to accept an error rate of 1 in 20, but I'm going to do five tests.' A 1 in 20 error rate shared over five tests is actually a one in four error rate! Suddenly your alpha is, in reality, 25% instead of 5%. By bundling up your dependent variables into one package and analysing them together, you avoid this problem, and the statistical formula is able to take into account the overlap between dependent variables caused by them being derived from one group of people, making your analysis more powerful.

ANCOVA

Analysis of covariance has two uses, which are really just versions of the same thing, but one is more of a cheat than the other. Hopefully that's got you reading on. I'd better explain what ANCOVA is now. Imagine that you have two independent variables (A and B), and you know that one of them (let us say A) is correlated with the dependent variable. You are mainly interested in the effects of B on the dependent variable, but in a way A is potentially muddying the waters, adding noise if you like. In a sense, A might be a confounding variable, although we don't normally call it that when we are doing ANCOVA. In fact, we call it a covariate, because it covaries with the dependent variable (a fancy way of saying that it correlates with it). The obvious solution to our little problem is to somehow take out the covariate from our ANOVA equation. That's what ANCOVA does. It essentially works out the effect of one variable on another, partialling out (see Chapter 6) the effects of the covariate. An example will help here.

The simplest form of ANCOVA is the one-way version, just as the one-way ANOVA itself is the most simple type. Imagine that I wanted to look at the effects of eating walnuts on memory. I have three groups eating either no walnuts, two walnuts a day or four walnuts a day. My dependent variable is the scores on a recall test given after 1 month. The walnuts contain omega-3 fatty acids, which I believe is good for the brain. However, I can't strictly control what other things the people in my groups eat, and omega-3 is also found in many other foods, but especially oily fish such as mackerel. Therefore, I ask people to keep a food diary, and at the end of the month I then know how much oily fish each person has eaten. As you would imagine, the oily fish eaten varies within and between groups. In each group I have some people who eat oily fish and some who don't, but there might also be more oily fish eaten in one of my conditions than in the others, which will interfere with my results considerably. What I do is run a one-way analysis of covariance, using oily fish consumption as the covariate. What the analysis does is 'remove' the effects of the oily fish by weighting the scores so that we see the effects of the walnuts shining through. This can have a rather dramatic effect on the scores. Sometimes an apparent difference can disappear, and sometimes a difference occurs where there would not have seemed to be one. Similarly, a trend can reverse, so that instead of groups' scores being in the order A–B–C they are now in the order C–B–A.

Furthermore, we can also consider what the means of the three groups are compared with what they might have been without the covariate interfering with them. It is possible to compute these estimated means, so we can imagine what scores we would have obtained if we had started with three groups of people who eat exactly the same amount of oily fish between them. Remember that this only works, however, when you have actually measured the covariate. This begs an important question. If you know in advance what a likely covariate is, why not make every effort to plan and sample your participants so that these things are controlled for in the first place? Well, that's exactly what you should do. Use analysis of covariance only when you are not in a position to control the covariate even though you can measure it. It should not be used when you want to save time or trouble planning your study properly. Always try to sample your population randomly, but, more importantly, work hard to randomly *assign* your participants to groups. As Howell (2007, p. 587) says 'The ideal application for an analysis of covariance is an experiment in which participants are randomly assigned to treatments (or cells of a factorial design). In that situation, the *expected value* of the covariate mean for each group or cell is the same, and any differences can be attributed only to chance, assuming that the covariate was measured before the treatments were applied.'

The second use of ANCOVA, which is the dubious one, is when its interpretation is stretched a little too far, although you'll find that this is commonly how it is employed in the literature. Some researchers use ANCOVA to make the claim that the dependent variable would be affected by the independent variable in a particular way if the covariate was kept constant. That is, this is what we *would* have found if everyone was scoring the same on the covariate. If you haven't fallen asleep yet, you'll probably see why this is going beyond the data in a rather unacceptable way. There's only one way to know what data or effects would have been in another situation, and that's to collect the data in the first place that allow you to draw the conclusion. Worse still, some people use ANCOVA in this way when there isn't a known relationship between the dependent variable and the covariate. Look out for this when you read research papers which rely on ANCOVA for their conclusions.

In case you were wondering, there is also, as logically there should be, such a thing as MANCOVA. I'll leave it to you to figure out what exactly it involves. I'm sure you can by now.

In this chapter we have run through the main types of ANOVA you are likely to need. The basics of analysis of variance are easy to understand, even though the more complicated forms of ANOVA are occasionally quite useless to researchers because the sets of interactions that they throw up are often uninterpretable. Moreover, complicated designs often fall foul of having too few participants. If you turn to the section on cell sizes, you'll see why. However, if you plan your analysis carefully, and you keep your eye on the problems that ANOVA can face, such as small cell sizes, lack of normality and so on, you should be able to tackle some fairly complicated research questions using your analysis of variance toolkit.

Σ CELL SIZES IN ANOVA DESIGNS

When you intend looking at lots of independent variables at once, you naturally would adopt a design that could be analysed by means of ANOVA. You must always try to resist the temptation to have lots of between-groups independent variables, because these act like knives, cutting your participant cake into many pieces. Bear with me on this: your total number of participants can be seen like a cake. Each piece of cake is a cell. Now, if you are interested in sex differences, half of your participants would normally be male, and half female. So, for 100 participants, you use the sex difference knife to cut it into two pieces, each representing 50 people. Now you have two cells, each with 50 participants. But, let's imagine you have another between-groups independent variable: age. For sake of argument, we can select four age groups, these being 10–19, 20–29, 30–39 and 40–49. Again, if you sample carefully, you ought to have exactly (or almost exactly) equal numbers of men and women in each age group. Each group of 50 participants is to be divided by 4, giving us 12.5 per cell. (I know you can't have half of a participant, but I'm doing this on purpose to make you think.) The age differences knife has cut each half into four more pieces. So, we currently have *eight* pieces of cake. Are you following this? If so, we'll make it more complicated and add another between-groups independent variable. How about family socioeconomic status? For the sake of this crude argument, we could divide this into three bands: 'lower', 'middle' and 'higher'. So now, each eighth of the cake is going to be divided into three pieces by the socioeconomic status knife. Each one will be a twenty-fourth of the whole. It gets very awkward now, because 12.5 divided by 3 gives us 4.17 (if you round up). That's how many participants we have in each cell of our design, based on 100 participants, and equal divisions created by each independent variable.

Let's try one more independent variable just to hammer home the point. IQ score will do the job. Again, we'll have three groups: 'higher', 'middle' and 'lower'. The IQ knife cuts each piece (cell) into three more pieces. So, that's 4.17 divided by 3, giving 1.39. Hopefully, you are now starting to see the problem. We have 100 participants, and just four independent variables or between-groups factors. It doesn't sound like a problem, but it really is. We have ended up with cell sizes (cake pieces) which are very small. Not only might the cake not feed a mouse, but the number of participants in each cell will certainly not feed the hungry ANOVA. Depending on which statistician you believe, the minimum acceptable cell size is somewhere between about 7 and 10. In our example, we have 1.39! How, exactly, can 1.39 people adequately represent a particular section of the population? It's virtually impossible.

Of course, this is based on a false premise, since we know that you can't have 1.39 people in a cell; you must have *whole numbers*. What this means is that, somewhere in the cake-cutting process, at least one knife slipped. Maybe more than one knife slipped. We really are likely to have different-sized pieces of cake, or what statisticians call unequal cell sizes. There might be 12 females with higher IQ who are from the lower socioeconomic status group and who are aged between 20 and 29, but, for example, only one male who is from these last three groups. Therefore, one male's scores might be matched against the average of the scores from 12 females in a particular cross-section of the data.

Small cell sizes and unequal cell sizes can both present big problems for analysis of variance. Put these problems together and you have more than double the difficulty. It's not hard to understand how. After all, ANOVA is analysis of *variance*. If you want to analyse variance between groups compared with variance within groups, you need to actually have some variance to analyse! How can a cell containing one participant actually contain any variance? One person has one score. The variance is zero. The standard deviation is zero. Trying to compare that with a cell containing 12 people with *some* variance (no matter how much) is simply not acceptable.

To follow through our example design with four between-groups factors, we can work out roughly how many participants we would need by multiplying back from our acceptable minimum cell size. Let's say we are happy with 10 participants per cell. If the cake gets cut into totally equal pieces, we will need 10 times the number of cells. The total number of cells is $2 \times 4 \times 3 \times 3$ (sex, age, socioeconomic status, IQ), i.e. 72. Pause and reflect on this for a moment. If you think you can carry out a study with variables like these, you may need a *minimum* of 720 participants. Many professional researchers are generally only happy with around 20 participants per cell, so you can double that figure! Are you weeping yet?

So, let this be a lesson to you. Don't design studies which have lots of between-groups variables, and, if you must, make sure that you have enough participants to cope with it. Even then, don't expect anyone to ever be able to make sense of the results.

Σ SPHERICITY

Sphericity is a difficult concept to describe in words. Sadly, the pictures one might use to help to explain sphericity are also too complicated! However, it is important, because repeated measures ANOVA assumes sphericity, and so, if you haven't got it, your ANOVA needs tweaking. Clear? OK, this won't do as an explanation, I realise. Essentially, sphericity is a kind of homogeneity of variance within conditions of your ANOVA. Conditions, of course, are formed by the different levels of the variables acting at levels of other variables. We can also call these ANOVA cells, if you wish. It's all about comparing like with like. We might be looking for differences between cells, but these differences should really be differences only in the means, not in the standard deviations. SPSS automatically computes sphericity for you, and you should check Mauchly's test of sphericity every time you run this kind of ANOVA (i.e. repeated measures). If Mauchly's test comes out with a significant statistic, that means that there is a significant difference between a hypothetical spherical set of data and the data you actually have. At least, that's possibly the best way of looking at it. If this is the case, you can't assume sphericity. That's why SPSS gives you F-ratios calculated for 'sphericity assumed' and then bails you out if you can't do that by calculating the F-ratios another way which takes sphericity into account. So, in conclusion, check Mauchly's test, then select the correct F-ratio for your analysis. SPSS gives you the common corrections for sphericity, the Greenhouse–Geisser and the Huynh–Feldt corrections. Generally speaking, the Greenhouse–Geisser correction is the best to take. You end up with degrees of freedom that are not whole numbers, which might seem strange at first glance, but you need not worry yourself with how and why. Both of these corrections are quite conservative, so be warned that you might find an effect 'disappearing' when you look down from the first line of your ANOVA table to the next.

Another way to check for sphericity is by ignoring Mauchly's (which works only properly in certain conditions), and to simply compare the F-ratios given to you from the different corrections that SPSS computes. You're OK if they all yield pretty much the same numbers, but if the corrected versions differ considerably from the uncorrected one you can't assume sphericity and you should use a corrected version. Obviously, this is especially important if your standard calculation of the F-ratio shows a significant effect but the corrected versions do not.

Σ ROBUSTNESS OF ANOVA

Robustness refers to the extent to which a test can still do its job when you feed it wonky data. Very robust tests don't lose much power when you break their assumptions. Less robust ones dramatically lose power the moment you use the wrong kind of data. You'll be pleased to learn that ANOVA is actually quite robust. ANOVA can open with moderate violations of normality. It tends to demand homogeneity of variance a little more, but even then you can break the assumption a little and still end up with a result you can have some confidence in. Some statisticians almost go as far as saying that we needn't bother with non-parametric versions of ANOVA at all. So, good old ANOVA, eh?

Σ FAMILYWISE ERROR

When we conduct a set of inferential statistical tests on data, each time we have error associated with it. The most worrying error, of course, is the type I error. It's disconcerting to think that we might be looking at a difference that doesn't really exist in the bigger world, and then basing our theories on it. Finding something that isn't really there is very dangerous. The trouble is, the more we look, the more the chances of finding a mirage increase. We conventionally set alpha, the level at which we reject the null hypothesis, at 0.05 or 5%. There is another way to think of this, that is 1 in 20. This means that we accept that the difference (or relationship) that we have observed could happen by chance alone 1 in 20 times. Any single time we perform a test, we are bearing that in mind. It could be the 1 in 20. However, we live with that, since 1 in 20 is small enough. Our observed effect is more likely to be 1 of the 19 in 20 which are 'real'. However, if we fix alpha at 5% and continue to run tests in a set, what happens when we have run 20 tests? Imagine if you needed to run 20 t-tests to look for differences between various means. Now, this sounds a lot, but it's actually not that rare a necessity. If you have a study involving sex differences, age differences (let's say just two groups, younger and older) and two types of puzzle for people to solve, then there are eight means. Grab a piece of paper and work out how many comparisons between means that gives you. You'll find that, in order to test every mean against every other one, you'd need 28 tests. Given an alpha of 0.05 each time, that means one–and-a-bit of your tests will show you something that might not be true. The problem is that you don't know *which* one-and-a-bit is wrong. So, effectively, it might be the one comparison you are basing all your theories on! Therefore, you might as well not bother.

So what has this got to do with familywise error? A set of tests that you carry out together are called a 'family'. Each test has an error rate attached to it, and so a batch of tests also has an error rate, called the familywise error rate. In order to avoid the problem I have discussed above, you should adjust the alpha level of tests you conduct in a family. There are various ways of doing this, but they all involve bringing down the error rate overall. Now, if you intend carrying out 10 tests, for example, you'll often find yourself having to adjust the alpha to bring down the error rate to an extent that you might find that, instead of an alpha of 0.05, you have one of 0.005. That's 0.5% instead of 5%. Each test therefore is much more conservative. (This adjustment is often called 'protection', by the way.) Of course, when you do this, you make it much more difficult to detect trends in your data because only the really strong ones can now show through. By protecting ourselves from type I error, we automatically and unavoidably increase the type II error rate. There's no way around this. If I have two bags, with five apples in each, and decide that I want 10 apples in one bag, and move five of them over, I end up with one empty bag. For those physicists out there, think of every action having an equal and opposite reaction. When you paint the wall, the paint in the can diminishes. Global warming actually means that something else is getting colder. Of course, it's the sun, since the sun makes us warm, and every day that the sun shines it gets a little colder, which is why eventually there won't be a shining sun at all. Don't panic; the burning out of the sun will occur a very long way in the future, and even if you're a slow reader I promise you will finish this book before it happens.

ANOVA is basically a way of controlling familywise error by clumping your *t*-tests together under one, extra-protected umbrella. However, what happens when you want to conduct further tests to investigate small differences between groups in your ANOVA? We call these further tests comparisons, and they can be planned in advance, or done on the hoof later. Either way, we need to protect ourselves against high familywise error.

Σ *A PRIORI* AND *POST HOC* TESTS

If you know any Latin, you will realise what *a priori* and *post hoc* mean. They translate, at least in our statistical arena, as 'in advance' and 'after the event', and refer to tests we conduct after we have the data. You might ask why we would do that. The answer is that we sometimes need to dig around to find the source of some complicated result, such as an interaction. In actual fact, *post hoc* tests are contrasted with *a priori* tests, which are planned prior to collecting the data, and so are always intended. You'll find that many research articles refer to *post hoc* tests when strictly speaking they should have been *a priori* ones, as you can usually predict which analysis you'll need. To complicate things further, you also hear talk of *planned* and *unplanned comparisons*. Basically, these pretty much add up to the same thing as *a priori* and *post hoc* tests respectively. Just to confuse things further, occasionally, *post hoc* tests are called *a posteriori* tests.

When you conduct a *t*-test to look for differences between just two sets of scores there is no need for any further analysis. That's because the *t*-test tells you that A is different from B. There's nothing more to explore. However, what happens in the case of a one-way analysis of variance, where, let's say, you have three groups to compare? This time, A, B and C are in play, and our overall ANOVA will tell us of there is a difference somewhere across the groups. *Somewhere* is the important word here. Quite simply, the ANOVA doesn't tell us where. We need a way of working out where that difference lies, either between A and B, B and C or A and C. We now need a further set of tests. In fact, you can theoretically do this with some *t*-tests. However, multiple *t*-tests are not recommended because they are built to be used once, and not a number of times. If you perform multiple *t*-tests, you run the risk of finding something just because you are looking too hard. There is a simple way around this, which is to protect *t* against error. In fact, by altering your level of alpha in advance of the tests, so that each test requires that much larger a difference before it detects it, you are doing something known as using *protected t*. Whenever you make these corrections, you are said to be being *conservative*. In fact, when tests are stringent and when you make it hard for yourself to detect the result you are looking for, we also call this conservativeness. Some tests are conservative by their very nature. The beauty of being conservative is that if you find something, it really is quite highly likely to be 'real'. However, you miss a lot this way that might be real too, but is simply small. It's like setting the resolution on a microscope to a different level.

There are a range of tests which will do this and statisticians argue over which to use and when. In essence, however, they all do very similar things, and what you need to know is that they are simply ways of testing each group against each other to pick out smaller differences from within an overall ANOVA term.

To cut an extremely long story short (there are entire books on *post hoc* tests), I have presented the most commonly used tests here.

Bonferroni's Correction

This conservative test is basically achieved by conducting a *t*-test and dividing the alpha by the number of comparisons you are making. So, instead of the normal 0.05, you assume a different cut-off point for judging significance. With two comparisons, you divide 0.05 by 2, to give you a new criterion of 0.025. For three, it is 0.016, for four 0.0125 and for five it is 0.01. Bonferroni's *t* can be used for planned or unplanned contrasts, and so is really the best to use most of the time. However, if you run this in SPSS, the program assumes that you want to run all possible pairs of tests, and adjusts the alpha accordingly. The problem is that there might be only three you are interested in out of a possible 10. So, instead of setting the alpha at 0.016, it is set at 0.005, making the type II error rate very high indeed. You can also make a Bonferroni correction when you are comparing means from a non-parametric analysis, but this time you adjust the alpha for Mann–Whitney *U* or Wilcoxon, depending on the non-parametric equivalent of ANOVA that you have used (which in turn, of course, depends on the design).

An even more conservative test, which you would want to use only when you really want to stamp down on error, is *Sheffé's t*. SPSS will compute this for you. It is so conservative, however, that differences that do exist in the real world are often not demonstrated by it. You end up with a high type II error rate instead.

Simple Effects Analysis

This involves breaking down interaction terms in ANOVA to find where the significant difference might lie. The simplest case would be in a 2×2 ANOVA, that is where there are two levels of each independent variable. You take the first independent variable, and select out of the data one of the two possible groups (for sake of argument we might select out the males, leaving the females). Then we look at the effect of the other independent variable on the dependent variable for females only by running a corrected t-test, or a one-way ANOVA. Then we do the opposite, taking out females, including only males, and running the analysis again. Now we know the effects of one independent variable on the dependent variable for each sex separately. Of course, that's only half of the story. If the other independent variable was age (young and old), we might now want to select out all the young participants, to check the effect of the sex on the dependent variable for only the younger participants. Then, the young are selected out, the old go back in, and we look at the effect of sex on the dependent variable for older participants only. Essentially, we end up with four tests conducted.

For an in-depth discussion of all of these and more, with precise detail on when you should use them and when you shouldn't, see Clark-Carter (2004).

6

CORRELATION AND REGRESSION

Correlation is a way of looking at the relationships between variables that we have measured. A special statistic, called a correlation coefficient, is a way of expressing the relationship between variable X and variable Y. Essentially, we compute correlation coefficients when we are interested in knowing what tends to happen to one score when another score increases. For example, we might want to know if taller people are also heavier people. Naturally, correlation is *always* about within-groups/repeated measures designs. We never refer to this, because strictly speaking this is a term used only for experimental studies, and correlation is not experimental. However, I'm sure you can see the point that I'm getting at; we can correlate scores with each other only when all scores have come from the same group of people. You cannot correlate measures derived from different populations. Scores must always come in pairs. You can't correlate the heights of a bunch of people from Scotland with the weights of a group of Albanians.

Correlation, as I said, is not a method of analysis that is tied up with experimental studies. What I mean by this is that taking scores from people by measuring something is all that you do. There is no manipulation of variables, no control of other variables. Simply, we measure things, and see if they relate to each other. We don't *do* anything to our participants. We are not looking at the effect of one thing on another. Precisely because of this, we must also never make the mistake of interpreting correlations in terms of cause and effect. It is appropriate to infer that something causes something else only if you have made it happen yourself. Just watching two things occurring and commenting on the fact that they seem to go together is not enough. Correlation is that kind of concept. We don't make people weigh a certain amount, and we don't make people grow to certain heights. These things exist already in some amount, and we simply measure them.

When we have our measurements, taken from a set of people, we can apply a statistical test of correlation to give us a sense of the strength of the relationship between the scores. This is called a *correlation coefficient*, and I will return to it in a little while. Remember: correlation is *co*-relation. That is, the concept is concerned with how things relate to each other.

The first thing to do if you want to see if two variables or measurements relate to each other is to plot them using a scatterplot. As you know, graphs have an X- and a Y-axis. Therefore, to keep this simple, let us imagine that we have two scores from a set of people; one is a measure of their ability to play the xylophone and the other is the number of times they have been yachting. (Forgive me, but I am quite lazy and this means I can label the axes X and Y and not have to explain anything more.) So, each person has a score on the measure of X and a score on the measure of Y. In a group of 20 people, there will be 40 numbers in total.

What we do is plot the X scores against the Y scores, putting a dot on the graph where a person's scores meet. Eventually, there will be 20 dots on the scatterplot, because each dot is a person. This is shown in Figure 6.1. As you can see, there is a person who has scored very low on both measures and a person who has scored very highly on both. There is also a person who has been yachting only once, but who is really quite good at playing the xylophone. Can you find them? Most of the people have an 'average' score on both measures, which is why there is a cluster of scores in the middle of the graph. You might also notice that there are actually only 19 dots. That's because two people in my dataset yielded the same scores, so in effect their dots are laid on top of each other.

Now, the shape of the cloud of dots allows us to get a sense of the nature of the relationship between the two variables or measures. When the dots are nicely packed together in a neat line, the relationship is strong,

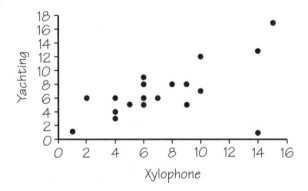

Figure 6.1 A scatterplot of yachting experience versus xylophone-playing expertise.

but when the cloud is very diffuse, looking more like a circular patch, for example, there is not really a relationship between the two variables.

Another way of looking at this is by drawing an imaginary line through the dots and then considering how close the dots are to the line. You need to put the line as close as possible to as many as the dots as possible. When the dots are close to the line, there is probably a high relationship between the variables, but when the dots are a long way away from the line, there probably isn't. This is why a circular cloud of dots will never represent a strong relationship. Too many dots are too far away from the line. Or, if you prefer, think of this a third way. A strong relationship between the variables measured means that it is quite easy to spot where the line would be drawn that best fits the data, or that is closest to the dots. However, when the relationship is poor or non-existent, you simply can't see where it would be best to draw a line. If you can't work out where to draw it, it's because there's really nothing to draw because there's no relationship worth speaking of between the two variables.

At school, you might have been asked to draw 'lines of best fit' through data represented graphically. I'm sorry to tell you that this is really quite wrong. Your teachers should never have expected that of you, unless you happen to have attended a school for geniuses. Drawing accurate lines of best fit is extremely difficult to do by hand, and some would say virtually impossible. Instead, we need some mathematical way of determining that line. This is partly why we have correlation coefficients, and don't just draw scatterplots and leave it at that.

For every line of best fit you might try to draw through a set of data points, there is another one just next to it that might be a bit better fit. And another one next to that. Are you sure that the one you drew was best? Usually, you can't be. So how can you be sure? Well, let us reflect on what a line of best fit actually means. It means a line that is *closest to most of the dots*. What does that mean? It means a line for which the sum total of the distances between the dots and the line is smaller than would be the case for any other line. So, you draw an imaginary line, then measure how far each dot is from that line. You square those distances and add them up. (You have to square them, because there are dots on each side of the line, which would mean that there were some minuses, and we don't want to add minuses to pluses.) Now, you can do the same with a different imaginary line, and so on. The line which gives you the smallest total squared distances is the true line of best fit.

Those distances between the line and the dots are called *residuals*. You will need to know this when you read about *multiple regression* later.

So, to get back to correlation, we tend to have a strong correlation when the residuals are very low, and a weak correlation when the residuals are very high. What a statistical test of correlation does is work out that best line with the lowest residuals for you, and to express that in terms of a number. That number is the correlation coefficient. It also takes into account how many people you have taken measures from. You'll see why soon.

Correlation coefficients vary from 0 to 1. When there is no relationship between two sets of scores, the correlation is said to be 0.0. A perfect relationship would be described by a correlation of 1.0 (or −1.0). A perfect relationship, by the way, is one in which all of the dots are exactly in a straight line and the total of the squared residuals is exactly zero. If you ever have this happen in real data in a study involving more than 30 participants, write to me. I am not expecting a flood of letters. I have never seen a perfect correlation with a reasonable number of participants, and neither has anyone I have ever worked with.

Most real-world correlations are somewhere between the two extremes of 0 and 1 (or 0 and −1). We tend to take seriously any correlation that is more than about 0.3, and we get very excited if we can show a relationship over about 0.8.

So what does this tell us? Well, a strong correlation tells us that, as one score changes, the other score changes in a mathematically predictable way. If a 5°C increase in temperature makes *every* person buy *two* more ice creams each month, the correlation between temperature and ice cream purchase would be perfect. This is because every time one thing happens, the other thing happens in a fixed way across all people. Of course, not everyone buys ice cream when it is hot. Some people can't face ice cream in hot weather and buy ice lollies instead. For those people, the relationship works the other way. Throw those into the equation, and it is much harder to see a pattern between temperature and ice cream purchase, because the graph you draw will show outliers (dots that don't fit the pattern). The correlation is thus reduced. Think back to that circular cloud showing a correlation of zero. One way of conceptualising this is as a depiction of a lot of outliers spread equally across the graph.

Until now we have been considering a situation in which the relationship between the two variables is positive. What I mean is that an *increase* in X is associated with an *increase* in Y. What happens when an increase in X is associated with a *decrease* in Y? We shouldn't dismiss this, because knowing that one thing goes down when another goes up is really just as useful as knowing that one thing goes up when another does the same. We don't disregard this; we call it a negative correlation. This time, the strength of the correlation varies between 0 and −1. Otherwise everything is exactly the same.

Figure 6.2a, b and c show a perfect positive, perfect negative and almost zero correlation respectively. Furthermore, Figure 6.2d and e show exact zero correlations of entirely different shapes. Can you see why these give correlations of zero? Remember, these are extraordinarily unlikely to ever occur in real data, but right now we are in theoretical mode, so that doesn't matter. Remember: a correlation of 0.8 is not stronger than a correlation of –0.8. They are of exactly the same strength. They simply work in different directions.

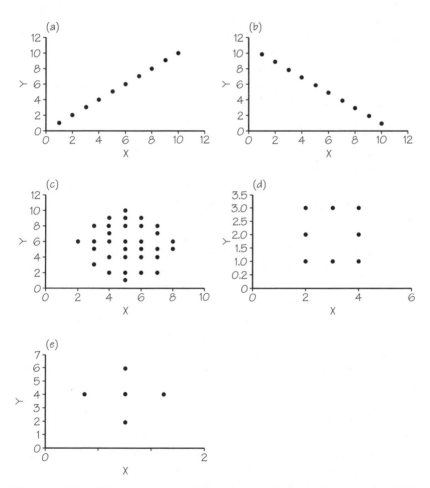

Figure 6.2 A, B, and C show a perfect positive, perfect negative, and almost zero correlation respectively. D and E show exact zero correlations of entirely different shapes.

You will have noticed that I have carefully used the term 'associated with' when I have been describing the relationship between variables in a correlation. This is because we must, at all costs, avoid suggesting that there is any causation. A rise in X does not necessarily cause a rise in Y. A decrease in X does not necessarily give rise to an increase in Y. We cannot know this. All we can say is that one thing seems to happen when another one does. Thus, it is *associated* with it. I attend various meetings, and there is always another gentleman at those particular meetings, no matter where they are held. Every time I am there, he is there. Every time he is there, I am there. So, is it fair to assume that we are the same person? Obviously, it is not! However, we are certainly associated with each other. Something else binds us together, and causes us to be in the same place at the same time. So it is with correlation. You must never assume that one thing is causing the other. Even if it were true, you can't know it. Why? Well, because firstly you aren't sure of the direction. Just because X is associated with Y doesn't mean that X causes Y. It could be that Y causes X. How are you going to know which way around it is? Even more likely, something else (call it P) causes R, then R causes both X and Y to occur. I know, it is complicated. Most things in life are.

Hopefully, by now, you have a good sense of what correlation is. It is important to consider a few more issues on this topic, though.

When you compute a correlation coefficient using a test of correlation, you end up with a P-value. This is expressed as a number between 0 and 1, just like the correlation coefficient itself. Please do not confuse these. I have seen many students do just that when interpreting the outputs from statistical packages such as SPSS. The correlation coefficient is a measure of how strong the relationship between the two variables is. The P-value is a sense of how likely you would be to get a correlation of that strength or greater, with that number of participants, if in the real world the two variables are not correlated whatsoever. So, a high value of the correlation coefficient, known usually as r, means that there is a strong relationship between the two values. A high value of P is a bad thing, however. It means that the result you have got is quite likely to occur even if the two variables are not actually correlated. So, ideally, you want high r and low P, and you've got a sound correlation on your hands.

When interpreting a test of correlation that you have computed, you must always look at three things. These are the scatterplot, the coefficient of correlation (r) and the P-value. If you look at only one or two of these, you will be highly likely to mess up your conclusions, and could look quite silly when a lecturer checks your results.

- Check the scatterplot! Does it look like there is a correlation there? If not, there probably isn't.
- Check the value of r! Is it strong enough? Below about 0.3 it is difficult to make any use of a correlation for most practical purposes or for building theory.
- Check the P-value! Is it below 0.05? If not, you do not have a statistically significant correlation on your hands, and you should not start to build theory on it.
- Look out for statistically significant correlations which have low r-values. This can happen. If you have a large sample size, a correlation of 0.1 can be statistically significant, but you won't see any obvious pattern on the scatterplot and you will find it hard to make use of it for the purposes of prediction or theory building. I'm being controversial here, but in my opinion the r-value and the scatterplot are most important. Unless these two measures tell a good story, the P-value is often just misleading. My advice to you, as a student, is to be wary of any statistically significant correlation that is weaker than about $r = 0.3$.
- Check your scatterplot for outliers that might sway the correlation towards looking stronger or weaker than it really is.

Sometimes, you will see on your scatterplot that a couple of people are displaying unusual results compared with the rest. With small sample sizes, outlying values can do dangerous things to the value of correlation coefficients that you compute. The line of best fit, as it were, can be swayed off in the wrong direction by some outlying values, to the extent that you seem to have a strong correlation when you don't, or vice versa.

Look at Figure 6.3. Here you can see that most scores seem to show little or no correlation between the variables. However, because the correlation takes all dots into account, the two dots at each end can trick you. They twist and pull the line of best fit and make the correlation appear stronger.

Look now at Figure 6.4. Here you can see that there is actually a fairly high correlation between the two variables. However, two people show strange scores. What their scores do is make the overall shape of the pattern of dots much more like a spread-out cloud than a nice, neat line. As we know, a cloud is what a low correlation looks like, so the effect of these people's scores is to lower the correlation.

I hope that you can now see that you should always look carefully at your scatterplot. Identify any aberrant values which could be swaying the value of r, and think about removing them from any analysis. This is not cheating, since you are making this decision based upon the data that you

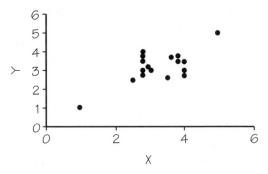

Figure 6.3 A very low correlation could be artificially made higher by outliers.

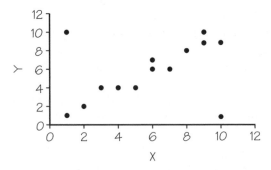

Figure 6.4 A high correlation could be artificially made lower by outliers.

have. If almost everyone fits a consistent pattern, except for one or two participants, then you should not allow those participants to completely alter the picture. Of course, there is a better way around this problem. With more and more participants, the chances of a couple of outliers denaturing the correlation is smaller and smaller. If in doubt, test more people (up to a point, that is!). If you can't, then consider trimming the data to remove clear outliers. It is always best if you can show the scatterplot to someone else and see if they corroborate your decision.

Σ PARTIAL CORRELATION

Simple correlations are very useful, but there are sometimes other questions that we would like to ask. A correlation matrix is simply a set of correlations computed separately and then stuck into a table. Each correlation in there is simply a single correlation, nothing more. What happens if we would like to know about relationships between correlations, as it were? Intercorrelations, as they are called, are important, because they can help us to build up an idea of the way that different variables interact with each other. Sometimes one correlation is really another in disguise. It sounds weird, I know, but let me explain further.

Let us imagine that I have computed correlations between three variables. They are number of hours a student spends on private study per week, the number of hours they spend watching TV and a measure on a test at the end of the week. So, we find that the raw correlations are as follows:

Private study with TV = -0.38
Private study with test score = 0.60
TV with test score = -0.45

Now, as you can see, private study is associated positively with scoring well on the test, as you'd expect. Also, watching TV tends to mean that people do less well in the test, and it seems that there is a trade-off between watching TV and private study, in that people can't do both at once, and so every hour spent watching TV is, of course, an hour *not* spent in private study. TV watching is, in a sense, getting in the way. If I want to know what the relationship between the test score and private study really is, I could do with taking out the interference of TV. What would the relationship be if everyone had watched the same amount of TV? Would it be different? Well, we can work this out using partial correlation. Partial correlations are so called because we can remove an additional, correlated factor from the equation, as it were. Because we know what all of the raw correlations are, we can squeeze one of them out. This squeezing out is really called partialling out, hence the term partial correlation.

An analogy might be useful here. Look at a piece of old furniture and you'll see that the carpenter has used a joint to keep two pieces of wood together. Carpenters know many ways of joining wood together, but we'll take a really simple example, one with fingers of wood which fit together like your fingers fit together if you hold hands with someone. You can see what I mean in Figure 6.5.

Of course, what if you can also see that the carpenter has added some glue to the joint, to make it that bit stronger? Now, we can't see how strong the joint is because the glue adds some strength. How strong would the joint be without the glue? Partial correlations allow us to get a sense of this.

Sometimes we can be very surprised what happens when we partial out a variable from a correlation. What happens isn't always what we expect.

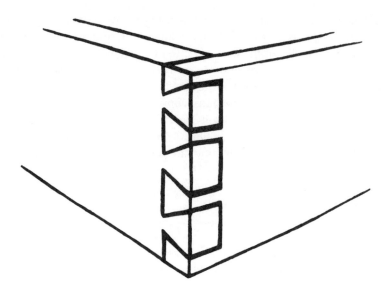

Figure 6.5 A dovetail joint.

The partial correlation can go up or down, and sometimes stay exactly the same. One thing to be aware of is that this is a little controversial because you are using your data to work out what something would be like if it wasn't like what it is! By working out a partial correlation in our example, we are saying that the correlation would be different if everyone had watched exactly the same amount of TV. There's only one sure-fire way of knowing what the correlation between test score and study time would be if everyone watched the same amount of TV. I think you know what that is. Yes, you'd need to collect data on people who are matched on their TV-watching behaviour. That is, you'd need to control that variable in the data you collect. So, my advice would be to use partial correlation carefully, and if it reveals that a relationship might be different if some other variable were controlled for, perhaps consider controlling for that variable in an add-on study, if resources and time permit.

You can't always control other variables, of course, and that's why partial correlations are used. If you are not able to restrict people's behaviour, then you might have to resort to using this particular statistical technique. An example of when it tends to get used is in medical or epidemiological studies. If you want to know about heart disease and smoking and drinking, for example, you simply collect data on these and then you can use partial correlation to tell you what the relationship between heart disease and drinking is when you take out the effects of smoking. You can't stop people smoking, so you need to do it this way. Of course, remember that you can partial out each variable in your correlation matrix in turn, giving you a whole set of partial correlations. You would look at not only the relationship between X and Y after partialling out Z, but also between Z and Y partialling out X and between X and Z partialling out Y.

Those of you who are reading this book in order should have noticed something very important, which is that the essential logic of partialling out is the same as that of including a covariate in an analysis of variance. Each time, we are removing the influence of A in order to see what B and C have got to do with each other.

Σ ATTENUATION OF CORRELATION

Whenever we calculate a correlation coefficient, we do so with a sample of the potential population we are interested in. We don't measure or test *all* people. In fact, this is a problem we have with all statistical tests that we perform. However, in the case of correlation, statisticians are particularly interested in the phenomenon of attenuation. Essentially, attenuation means 'shrinking' or 'dwindling', and it refers to the way in which a relatively small sample of data for a correlation tends not to have the same properties as a larger sample, mainly in terms of the scale used. If you measure something on a scale from 1 to 10, and then get data from 20 people, there's a good chance that you won't necessarily get a good range of scores from that small sample. In fact, if you think about it, a normally distributed variable measured from 1 to 10 will give you mainly scores in the middle and few if any at the ends of the scale. Because, in a correlation, you are measuring people on two *scales*, the problem applies twice. Now, a correlation is more sensitive if you have people with scores from all over the scales. It is best to have no 'gaps' in the data. If the distribution of our sample scores is such that they are all cramped up in one area of the scale, we can say that the data are attenuated. There are two ways to solve this problem. The best is to avoid it altogether by simply collecting enough data that the points on the scales are well sampled. There is, however, a controversial statistical technique known as correction for attenuation. What this method does, its fans claim, is tell you what the correlation would have been if you had a larger sample, having measured more people on your scales. Its opponents point out that you simply can't predict what something would have been, because a small sample doesn't necessarily tell you what a whole population is like. Equally, the assumption that modest correlations tend to get stronger with larger samples is true only some of

the time. Sometimes, they get weaker or disappear altogether. Therefore, you should always think twice about using a correction for attenuation.

Σ HETEROSCEDASTICITY

Whenever you conduct a correlation, and more importantly a multiple regression analysis, you should always check for heteroscedasticity. In fact, SPSS will calculate a test of it for you as part of a regression analysis, and it's crucial that you know what this means.

Although it is most pertinent to multiple regression, it's easier to explain scedasticity in the case of a simple bivariate correlation. When you draw a scatterplot of the relationship between two variables, look carefully at the plot. As you know by now, a strong correlation occurs when the residuals are low, that is when the dots are close to the regression line. Now, not only do you want a nice neat correlation with the dots close to the line, you want that to happen all the way along the line. What if it does not?

Imagine a scatterplot where all of the dots are close to the line for low values of the two variables, but more spread out for higher values of both. Or the opposite, with a tight relationship at the higher end but a loose one at the lower. Equally problematic is a nice close relationship 'spoiled' by a blob of looseness in the middle. You can see these represented below in Figure 6.6a, b and c.

When the relationship is not the same all the way along the line, we have what we call heteroscedasticity. Homoscedasticity is its opposite, when the residuals are same all the way along the line, or, in other words, the relationship holds up at all values of the two variables. As you can see, it is important to be aware of this because of the mess it creates when you apply tests which assume that the relationship between the variables is constant across all values. It's like trying to fit a square peg into a round hole; it might actually fit, but there could be very awkward gaps around it, and those gaps represent the information that you are missing when you run correlations and regression on data like this. Ultimately, like with all statistical tests, you only end up fooling yourself by feeding the wrong kind of data into them.

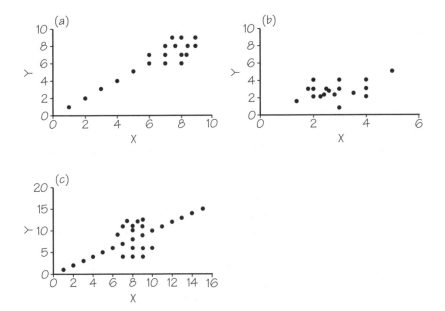

Figure 6.6 Types of heteroscedasticity.

Σ CRONBACH'S ALPHA

In my opinion, this is one of the most useful and important tests that we have. Student projects often feature a statement-based instrument of some sort, developed to test a particular thing, and containing a set of attitude statements which are intended to tap into that particular construct. For example, someone might develop a 10-item test of attitudes to obesity, or a dozen attitude statements on the subject of liking of statistics. In fact, let's imagine that this is just what we are doing. Here's my set of statements which I think tap into liking of statistics.

- I like nothing better than a Kolmogorov–Smirnov at the end of a long day.
- I cannot contain my excitement at the thought of kurtosis.
- If I met Mann and Whitney I'd shake their hands.
- There's nothing I wouldn't do for a Wilcoxon.
- ANOVA is my only source of satisfaction.
- The anticipation of a correlation is unbearable.
- I am impressed by skew.
- There's only one thing better than regression: multiple regression.
- Factor analysis means the world to me.
- *The Phi Coefficient* is my favourite film.
- I love the smell of fresh data.
- I just wish everything in life was as simple as path analysis.

Now, I am going to take this and give it to lots of people, and they will respond to each item using a Likert-type scale of agreement, and I will take those numbers, add them up for each person (or calculate the mean), and get a score that reflects their liking of statistics. Well, that's the theory. Of course, there's something I need to know before I can take the mean of all 12 answers. That is, are all the questions actually able to assess liking of statistics? What if some of them only *seem* as if they do? Do they items 'hang together', or are some of them actually outside of the scale? For example, it might be that liking of statistics is not at all related to liking of multiple regression. For some reason (we don't know why or how and it really doesn't matter right now), multiple regression might be a technique which people who generally like statistics have no feeling about whatsoever. It's unlikely, but it's possible. The last thing we want is a dud item diluting the power of our scale to detect what we want it to. Indeed, for all we know half of our items might be like this, and we certainly don't want to have 6 of our 12 items contributing to the mean score if they actually don't do what they think we do. This 'hanging together' of our items is called *internal reliability* or *internal consistency*, and we can measure it using Cronbach's alpha. It would be quite difficult to compute alpha without software to help us, but luckily SPSS will do it for us. First of all, don't get confused between Cronbach's alpha and other kinds of alpha (especially the rejection region that we use for testing hypotheses in inferential statistics, which is usually 5%). This is a different kind of alpha, and indeed this is not a test of significance at all, and the alpha we end up with has no *P*-value associated with it.

Now, the most obvious way to see if all of the items belong together in a scale is to see how they correlate with each other, and Cronbach's alpha is really a way of doing that, but a basic correlation matrix won't do, and actually would be very difficult to interpret if we had, say, 50 items, because the table produced would have too many cells in it! We couldn't see it on screen, and it would be so large that we could fill a wall with it.

Instead, Cronbach's alpha reduces this down to an overall alpha for the scale. This is *usually* a number between 0 and 1, and the nearer to 1 it is, the more we can be sure that the items are testing the same basic thing. I said usually, because technically alpha can range from 1 through to minus infinity, although we usually hope we never see a minus alpha, and certainly not one that is negative and too large. So, in a sense, you interpret alpha just like a correlation, with values between 0 and 1 representing the strength of the relationship between items. Unlike correlation, there's no *P*-value. Instead, we simply use a rule of thumb to judge whether the value is acceptable. Statisticians and researchers do argue about what is acceptable, but generally anything below 0.6 is dubious. Above 0.7 and it's looking good, and around 0.8 is probably ideal. Why not 0.95 or 0.99 or 1? Well, think about it. When alpha gets too large, it means that all of the items correlate with each other almost perfectly. This in turn means that each person is giving you the same response to each item. This begs the question why you need all of the items. With an alpha of 1, we have perfect agreement across all of the items. What this tells you is that you can simply choose one item and use that and only that. The rest of the scale is redundant. So, high but not too high is the answer.

So what is alpha doing? Well, it's not actually calculating all of the correlations between all of the items and then averaging them. What it is doing (although this is a lie, and I'll explain later) is averaging all of the possible split-half reliability correlations. What's that?

Split-half reliability correlations are the result of splitting the set of items in two, taking the total score for each person from each half, and then correlating the two totals. So, we might take 1, 2, 3, 4, 5 and 6, and total the responses for each participant. Then we take 7, 8, 9, 10, 11 and 12 and do the same. Of course, that's only one split half. There are many more, for example:

1, 3, 5, 7, 9, 11 and 2, 4, 6, 8, 10, 12
1, 2, 4, 5, 7, 8 and 3, 6, 9, 10, 11, 12
1, 2, 3, 10, 11, 12 and 4, 5, 6, 7, 8, 9

You get the idea? OK, now once you get your set of split-half correlations, you average them, and that's your alpha. Now, I did say I would explain why this is a lie. Actually, Cronbach's alpha is a way of short-circuiting this process, so you don't actually need to do this, but you end up with a figure of alpha that is mathematically equivalent.

Now how does this help us spot which items don't belong in the scale, so we can remove them? The beauty of a statistical program like SPSS is that it can also calculate many other alphas at the click of a button. SPSS can tell you what the overall alpha would be if you removed any individual item. There's a dialogue box which you can select for "'Scale if item deleted', which gives you just that for each item. I'm not going to tell you how to work out alpha, because I want you to learn properly, so look in the SPSS help menu, and you'll find an explanation of the right buttons to press.

Each time you run a Cronbach's alpha, you get an overall alpha value and the alpha you would get if each item was removed. You look for the largest alpha in the 'would-be' set, and then run the analysis again with that item removed. You must do this over and over again, separately for each item you want to remove. You can't just select a bunch of items and remove them all at once, because the alphas all change each time you run the analysis. You end up making a decision as to when to stop, which, as I say, is probably somewhere around the 0.8 mark, if you can achieve it. You have to balance this against the slowly dwindling number of items left in the set. Eventually, you will probably find that the alpha stabilises, and removing further items makes no appreciable difference. In fact, you might even reach a point where removing further items makes the alpha *decrease.*

Whenever you construct an attitude instrument, you should pilot it and run Cronbach's alpha to see if you can fine tune the instrument before using it properly. I'd also advise using Cronbach's alpha on 'off-the-shelf' instruments too. They often have a published alpha, and you can detect if there is something odd about your data (and perhaps your sample population) if your alpha is much lower than the published one. Don't just rely on what the authors tell you; test things out for yourself.

Σ REGRESSION

When correlation is used for the purposes of prediction, it is a special case which we call regression.

Σ MULTIPLE REGRESSION

As we have discussed earlier, correlation is also a form of something called regression. Furthermore, correlation can be used very nicely for predicting one score from another. If scores are related, we can estimate one of them when only one is available. This in itself is quite limited, because in life most things are multivariate. What I mean by this is that any one decision or behaviour that a person makes or engages in is likely to be affected by, or related to, a variety of factors, rather than just one. If we really want to predict whether someone is likely to be able to give up abusing alcohol, for example, we would probably need to know about when they drink, why they drink, if their parents were problem drinkers, how easily they can afford alcohol, and so on. Correlating each of these separate variables, one by one, with the intention to give up drinking can only take us so far. Firstly, it gives us the statistical problem of familywise error rates when we conduct multiple correlations. But, and more importantly perhaps, the other difficulty is that this won't tell us what the *combined* prediction of all of the factors can give us. It also doesn't tell us if we can dispense with some factors because they don't tell us anything that another factor can. What if social drinking behaviour predicts intention to give up, but also affordability does? It might be that social drinking behaviour and affordability are very closely related in themselves, and in fact there's no need to know about both because one will do the job of prediction.

Clearly, we need a way of bundling together a set of factors and looking at how they work together to predict something else. This is exactly what multiple regression does. In multiple regression, we have a set of predictors, and we have a predicted value, which is sometimes called a dependent variable, although I personally prefer it when the term 'target' or 'criterion' variable is used, because it takes us away from the confusing language of dependent and independent variables reserved largely for experimental studies. So, we use predictors to predict a criterion.

It's analogy time again. We are in darkness, and there is a target in the darkness that we want to illuminate. Our task is to light up all of the target (or as much as possible). We have a number of spotlights we can switch on, but we have been told that we must use only the minimum amount of electricity to achieve our goal. What do we do? Well, the sensible thing to do is to switch on the lights, one by one, each time noting how much of the target we can light up. If a spotlight does not light the target at all, forget it. We concentrate on the others. Now, imagine that each spotlight can shed *some* light on the target, but none of them can light it up completely. That means that we will need some combination of lights in order to complete the task. We need to make a note of how much each light can contribute to the overall illumination of the target, perhaps by turning them off and on, and trying them in different combinations. We might find that one light in particular can illuminate half of the target, but another light seems to do exactly the same. That is, two lights are able to light up one half (the same

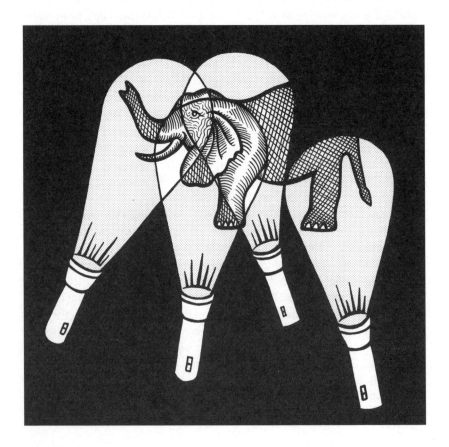

half) of the target. OK, so the obvious thing to do is to ditch one of them, because there's no point wasting electricity lighting the upper half of the target twice! Eventually, we might be able to light up 80% of the target using a combination of three spotlights, having dumped another three.

Back to multiple regression: the lights are the predictors, of course, and the target is the target variable or criterion. So what is the light? Well, the light on the target is the amount of variance in the criterion that we can predict or explain using the predictors. When we have our final combination of spotlights giving us maximum possible illumination, we have what is called a 'regression model'. We model variance in the criterion using the other variables. Modelling variance simply means that we are able to predict and explain the nature of a set of scores using other scores. That's exactly what happens in a correlation, but this time there are multiple variables doing the job.

Now to the detail of the statistics. When we conduct a multiple regression analysis, we need some way of seeing, at a glance, what the 'strength' of the model is. Just as we need to know if a difference is significant, or a correlation is significant, we also need to know if a model is significant. We also need to know the strength of the prediction in the same way that we know this when we conduct a correlation from looking at the value of r. Multiple regression analysis yields up a number of important figures, the first of which is the multiple correlation coefficient, generally known as R. This is just like a simple correlation coefficient, in that it varies between 0 and 1. The bigger the value, the better the prediction achieved by the model. Of course, this isn't a nice, simple, easy-to-visualise, two-dimensional correlation. You can't draw a simple scatterplot to show this relationship. For each predictor variable in your model, you add another dimension in mathematical space. So instead of a line of dots on a piece of paper, you really have a line moving through mathematical space in a way that human beings can't really 'see' in their heads. It's precisely because you can't easily see it that you need to rely on the numbers to tell you what is going on. You see, statistics are almost always there to help you, not to make life difficult, no matter what you sometimes feel! If you think of a normal scatterplot as being two-dimensional, then if you add one more predictor it is three-dimensional. Another predictor essentially gives you four dimensions and so on. Can you see the problem? Instead of a line of best fit, we really have a plane of best fit, cutting through space in a way that is too difficult to visualize.

Therefore, we look at the overall, multiple correlation coefficient and interpret it in the same way as a simple correlation, even though the process of getting there is much more complicated. Of course, being a sophisticated technique, there's much more to look for in our statistical output tables. The next step is to ignore the multiple R and now to focus instead on something called the R-squared and adjusted r^2. If we square R we get a measure of the variance that the combination of predictors explains in the target or criterion. Again, this varies between 0 and 1. However, this can be an optimistic figure, and SPSS output tables include a very important figure which is possibly the most crucial. This is the adjusted r^2. Adjusted why? As you know by now, small number of participants can be a bad thing. Also, fishing around for significance can also be dangerous. If you stick a bucketful of predictors into a regression model, chances are you'll find something, but it might not be meaningful. Therefore, the adjustment involves moving the R-squared value downwards to take into account the ratio of predictor variables to participants. Ideally, if you want many predictors in your model, you need lots and lots of participants. Therefore, levels of the adjusted r^2 are generally lower than the level of R-squared. If not, something might be amiss, and you should look carefully into this.

The beauty of the adjusted r^2 is that you can use it to get a direct measurement of the percentage of variance in the criterion that the model explains. All you have to do is move the decimal point. Therefore, a value of 0.34 gives you 34% of variance, 0.01 just 1% of variance, and 0.89 a whopping 89%. Generally speaking, any prediction above 20% is worth treating seriously, and anything above 40% is a clue to something quite exciting going on. If you can get above 70% prediction, that's really quite amazing, and rarely found in psychological literature.

What I haven't mentioned yet is statistical significance. You might wonder how we know whether the amount of variance we are able to explain is a significant amount. We can do this, because the model is tested using an F-ratio, just as in the case of analysis of variance. Now, as you know, analysis of variance compares variances between groups of data, and compares that with error variance. So, in the case of multiple regression, what exactly is being compared with what? Well, essentially, you have a plane of best fit that describes the relationship between the predictors and the criterion. If you think back to our discussion of correlation, I explained the notion of residuals. These are the gaps between the plane of best fit and the actual data points on the scatterplot. Well, the ANOVA test in multiple regression essentially uses the residuals as the error variance. It compares a hypothetical flat plane (a multiple correlation coefficient with the value of zero) with the regression plane in the model.

So, let's imagine that you have run a multiple regression, and the model predicts a significant amount of the variance in your target. You have an R, an adjusted r^2, an F and a P. What next? Something missing is the nature of the contribution that each individual predictor makes to the overall regression model. Which predictor is the strongest? Which is adding the least explanation of variance? We can access this information from another part of the statistical output tables. In SPSS, you will find a table which contains information on what are called unstandardised and standardised coefficients. You will find that each of your predictors in the model is listed separately. This table can tell you the individual contribution that each predictor makes to the model. The unstandardised coefficients (called B) tell you about the relationship between each predictor and the criterion in terms of actual amounts measured in the units we have in our data. Therefore, for example, if we are using vocabulary score and number of siblings to predict mathematics score, we can look at the B-values for these two predictors. If the B-value is for vocabulary score is 0.22, this means that for every point people get in the mathematics test they get 0.22 points in the vocabulary score. If we have a B of 0.02 for siblings, it means that for every point on the mathematics score people obtain, they have 0.02 siblings. Obviously, this is a tiny number because people tend not to have hundreds of siblings! You can check that each of these relationships is significantly predictive by looking at the t- and P-values that come with this. However, this is all a bit confusing as everything is measured in the units we started with. Wouldn't it be nice if we could compare on a like-for-like basis, using some kind of standard measure that means that each predictor can be compared with another in equal terms? Yes, you guessed it, of course. We have that too. Not only that, but it's an example of what we actually use z-scores for. If you conduct a multiple regression analysis in SPSS you will see from the output that there is also a column containing standardised coefficients, called beta values. This time, we have standard deviation changes listed in the column. For every one standard deviation that the criterion changes, a predictor changes by X standard deviations. This allows you to compare them directly with each other, as we are no longer bound by the problems associated with different units of measurement.

One word of caution. Don't mistake B for beta. I know it's easy to do, and most of us probably wish that the 'founding fathers' of statistics had come up with some more easily distinguishable terms, but they didn't, so we have to live with it.

So far we have dealt with the case of multiple linear regression, but there are some other forms of regression that you should be aware of, although there is not room here to go into detail.

When I told you about the targets and the spotlights, I lied a little. The analogy works only in part, because in a normal multiple regression you stick all of the spotlights on at once and work out their contribution to lighting up the target that way. Of course, that doesn't work properly. Sorry. In fact, there is a form of regression in which you can, indeed, stick spotlights on, one by one, to see how much the target lights up. This is called forward stepwise regression, and it allows you to build up a model, step by step. It is useful for testing predictions of which predictors will be the most useful and so on, because you can put them in first. Eventually, you stop adding variables because the new predictors don't really add anything to the explanation of variance in the criterion. Backward stepwise regression starts with you putting everything in, and then taking them out, one by one.

All of this assumes one thing: that the relationship between the predictors and the criterion is a linear one. That is, the line of best fit is a straight line, or, rather, the plane of best fit is a flat plane. What happens if it isn't? What happens if it is a U-shaped curve, or a sine wave, or something else? Well, firstly, multiple linear regression doesn't work. In fact, it will mislead you no end. There are some rather more complicated techniques for dealing with non-linear regression equations, and you can read about them if you want to in more advanced books on statistics.

Things to Keep an Eye On

Like all statistical tests, multiple regression makes certain assumptions about the data, and if you cheat by breaking the rules you can drastically cut down the usefulness of the technique, often to the point where you might as well not have bothered.

Sample Size

It's no surprise that a large sample is a good idea, and this is something that you should always bear in mind before you plan any study. Different authors of statistics textbooks suggest different rules of thumb for determining the minimum sample size for multiple regression. Dancey and Reidy (2002) suggest at least 15 participants for each predictor you're throwing into the model. Coolican (2004) cites a rule of 50 participants more than the number of predictors (so if you had 10 predictors you'd need at least 60 participants), although he also suggests that this is a minimum and that you should ideally have as many participants as possible. Possibly the most commonly used rule of thumb is that found in Tabachnik and Fidell (1996), who state that the number of participants needed is *at least* 50 plus the number of predictors multiplied by eight. With four predictors, you'd need, therefore, 36 plus 50, that is 86. Remember, however, that this is a minimum, and depends on the power that you hope to attain. In fact, you can calculate how many you need using a power analysis.

Multicollinearity

This is when your predictors correlate highly with each other. It's not a good thing for multiple regression. It's perfectly fine for your predictors to correlate with the criterion, in fact without that relationship you'd be hard pushed to end up with a significant model of variance prediction. However, when your predictors are related to each other above a certain degree, trouble can occur. This is called multicollinearity. You can check your raw correlation matrix to test this out, and perhaps you might need to remove predictor variables which have high correlations with other predictors. You might now wonder what a 'high' intercorrelation is? This is debated amongst statisticians, but generally anything about 0.7 is suspicious and above 0.8 is very problematic. You really should remove predictors that achieve correlations with other predictors at this level. SPSS will compute collinearity statistics for you as part of a regression analysis. A statistic for something called 'tolerance' gives you this. If the tolerance statistic is near zero, you might have problems with multicollinearity, whereas if it is not, perhaps over 0.5, you are probably safe.

Outliers

Multiple regression analysis can easily be thrown off track by outliers, that is scores which are some distance away from the general trend indicated by the line of best fit. This is for the very same reason that we have to be careful in correlation to avoid missing aberrant scores on our scatterplot. SPSS will work out something called Mahalanobi's distance, which is a statistic that detects outliers. However, you can usually find these by plotting the standardised residuals against the standardised predicted values (SPSS will again do this for you).

Normality

Multiple regression assumes normality in your variables, both predictors and targets. Non-normal variables should be excluded from the analysis. In actual fact, it is normality in the residuals that is important, but you will find that many people simply check the variables themselves. This is contentious, and you should be aware of this.

Linearity

For the reasons I've already given, multiple linear regression requires that the predictors are linearly related to your criterion. If not, the predictive value of the model is much reduced. Check the scatterplots for each correlation between predictor and criterion, and anything other than a straight line is worrisome. Curves, no. Camel humps, no. Straight lines or nothing at all.

Σ LOGISTIC REGRESSION

Since multiple regression is firmly rooted in the use of normally distributed continuous variables, you might have wondered how you would look at dichotomous, categorical variables if you still wanted an analysis that would allow you to predict variance in one variable from a set of others. In fact, just as there are non-parametric equivalents for most tests, there is also a form of regression that will allow you to deal with variables almost all of which are dichotomous (e.g. male/female, day/night). In many respects, performing logistic regression and understanding what it tells you is not drastically different from understanding and interpreting ordinary multiple regression, so I won't go into detail here. Now that you know that logistic regression exists, you know what to find out more about should you ever need it, and, more importantly, you won't try using standard multiple regression on a set of dichotomous variables.

7

FACTOR ANALYSIS

Factor analysis is one of the most complicated and confusing things you will probably ever meet with in your entire statistical life. That's why it tends to come towards the end of your formal teaching in statistics. To understand it involves building ideas upon ideas upon ideas, and keeping them in your mind as you move to the next stage, as it were. So, if you get lost in this section of the book, don't panic. You won't be the only one. I'll make this as simple as I possibly can, but you might need to re-read it a few times to keep track.

The first thing to understand is what factor analysis can do, and with what kind of data. If I told you that factor analysis allows us to figure out factors via statistical analysis, you wouldn't be surprised. But what are factors? Factors of what? Well, the second question is easy to answer glibly. They are factors of a construct. So now you might ask what I mean by 'construct'. A construct is an idea, if you like, but more than that. Constructs are ideas that you reify (make real) by thinking them up. The best and most obvious example is intelligence. Intelligence is real enough, in the sense that some people are more capable than others, it seems, but when we want to do something with the idea, we have do decide exactly what constitutes intelligence and what does not, and we base all of our theories on that definition. Everything then follows from that original construct. Another example of a construct is love. Another, perhaps, squeamishness. Note that none of these things is tangible. Constructs are, by their very nature, nebulous, and their nature and existence is almost always a subject of considerable debate.

OK, so, now you know what a construct is, you can consider factors. Factors are the theoretical units that make up a construct. Because constructs are big ideas with far-reaching consequences, they break down into smaller ones, and the smaller ones we call factors. In our example of intelligence, factors might include verbal ability, visuo-spatial ability, emotional intelligence, numerical ability, and so on. In the case of love, factors might include familial love, sexual love, love of animals, love of self, love of humankind, and so on. If we wanted to assess someone's capacity to love, we'd probably have to look at all of these. Someone who was a very high scorer on our construct of love would probably love everyone and anyone to some degree. A very low scorer might love no-one but themselves. Can you see why we need to look at the factors of a construct?

As you might realise, not only is the construct itself occasionally little more than idea, the factors are made up by the researcher. Usually they are based upon previous research or sound common sense, but they are still, from the point of view of critics, made up. Who is to say that something exists, and that not only does it exist but that it has a number of component parts, namely factor X, factor Y and factor Z? It sounds as though anyone conducting this kind of work is on very thin ice. Well, they are, but the beauty of factor analysis is that it can help to confirm what they believe in. Once they have data, factor analysis can be performed, and it can help to reject or support their assertion that construct P is made up of five factors, G, H, I, J and K. This is the first way that we can use the statistical technique. We call this *confirmatory factor analysis*. We have our ideas, and the technique helps us to sift the evidence and to confirm our ideas. So, we guess which fish are in the sea, then we cast our net out for a while, and check to see if we were right. This form of factor analysis is, as you can see, hypothesis driven.

The more controversial form of factor analysis, which is really a method of digging around in data to see what you can find, we call *exploratory factor analysis*. We simply cast our net into the sea, and then look what it turns up. This is a difficult approach, since statistically all sorts of meaningless patterns can emerge when you have a lot of data in front of you. Have you ever laid awake at night staring into the darkness, and then noticed patterns in the pitch black? People moving around, or birds or faces? It's often what makes children afraid of the dark. Alternatively, stare at a blank wall. After a while, you'll probably start to see things on it. Just faint images, but most people will see something. Of course, these things aren't real, but they look it. The same thing happens when you have a lot of data and you run big analyses on it. Trends or patterns emerge, but they aren't necessarily 'real' or replicable.

So, what is factor analysis doing to pick out patterns? Essentially, it is detecting clusters of correlations between variables. We throw in scores obtained from a batch of people on a number of measures, and it picks out relationships between those scores. Of course, it's much more complicated than that.

When we measure variables, such as responses people give to a set of attitudinal statements, those responses or variables have a special name in factor analysis. These are called *manifest variables*. They are the things that we measure. 'Manifest' as an adjective means that they are observable. We can see them. They are columns in our dataset, they are real measurements we have taken. (The word 'manifest' as a noun means 'a list of things'. Its most common use is in aviation. The passenger manifest is a list of all the people on board the aircraft.) However, hidden underneath those variables might be other, more conceptual variables (factors) which we don't directly measure. Combinations of particular questions we ask or measurements we take might together form a new kind of variable. We call these *latent variables*, because we can't them see or detect in a spreadsheet, and we haven't directly measured them. Factor analysis is commonly used to study personality. Imagine that we ask people to respond on a Likert-type scale to a series of statements, which are all about crime. Examples might be:

- Crime is becoming a problem in this country.
- Most of the time I feel safe when out and about.
- I am worried about crime.
- I do everything I can to protect my home.
- The police have too much to do.
- Crime doesn't worry me.
- Drugs are ruining society.
- We are not safe on the streets.
- I think people overestimate the incidence of crime.
- We must do more to reduce crime.

What factor analysis does is find the latent variables lurking in the manifest variables.

So how does it work? Well, one way to look at this is by converting the relationships between our variables into degrees, in a geometric fashion. Just as we have a correlation, we can talk about the angle formed between two variables. We allow the angles to vary between 0 and 90, just like we work out correlations between 0 and 1 (or −1 and +1, of course). When two variables are measuring the same thing, they are correlated perfectly. At this point, they are doing the same thing. Therefore, they have no separation between them. Thus, a correlation of 1 gives us an angle of 0 degrees. Two trains, running at the same speed on parallel tracks, side by side. Now, what is the furthest away they can be? After all, a correlation of zero means the variables have no relationship at all between them. They are different things, or if you like different trains going in very different directions. Well, if you think of the 360 degrees in a circle, you might be tempted to say that the furthest away they can be is 180 degrees. That is, they are going in opposite directions. However, if you think about it, the trains running away from each other are actually going to meet head on round the other side of the earth. They are actually on the same track, but they are going in different directions. So, if that happens in a correlation we actually call it a negative correlation, i.e. in this case −1. A perfect relationship running the other way. In actual fact, the worst relationship would actually be when the trains are running perpendicular to each other. That is, at a 90 degree separation. One train is running pole to pole and the other one is running on a track around the equator. Most of the time the trains are nowhere near each other. When the angle is 90 degrees, we have a correlation of zero.

OK, so now we have our trains running on the tracks. Let us imagine that we have our two trains, and one is the *Violence Express* and the other is the *Hatred Pullman*. They are running on tracks separated by an angle of 40 degrees, which actually corresponds to a correlation between them of 0.77. So, between them we can draw another angle, which is exactly halfway. Now we have a new angle of 20 degrees. This is what they have in common, if you like. We can also imagine that this is shared variance, just as we have discussed in the case of regression. This 20-degree angle is the line of best fit, again like in regression. If you were travelling on a third train, on this 20-degree track, you'd always be the same distance from either track, no matter where you were. Now, what train would run on this line? Well, something that described the *Violence Express* and the *Hatred Pullman* and what they have in common. So, now we have the *Angerstar*. So, what we are saying is that what violence and hatred have in common is anger.

What we now have is two variables and a factor. The *Angerstar* is the factor train. Now the *Violence Express* and the *Hatred Pullman* also are a certain angle from the *Angerstar*. That angle can also be converted back to a correlation, and in this case 20 degrees converts to a correlation of 0.94. The amount of relationship between a variable and the factor is referred to as the *loading* that the variable has on that factor.

Now it gets tricky. Up to now, I have said we have just two variables with one factor. Of course, when using factor analysis we are normally dealing with a lot of variables, often dozens. Each one is on a track, and there are potentially many factors which describe the relationships between different variables. This is like the real world, in that there are hundreds of thousands of trains running on many tracks. When we get to this level, we can't easily imagine all the angles and correlations and the factors between them all. In fact, they run in many dimensions, which makes it even more complicated. In life, trains run in only two dimensions, effectively, since the tracks are fixed. OK, the trains do go up and down hills on those tracks, so we can call it three dimensions if you like. Now, the factor analysis will work out relationships and angles between variables which go beyond three dimensions. Imagine a world with seven or 12 dimensions, and then you have the world of the statistics behind factor analysis. (Except, of course, you can't imagine a world with those dimensions because you have no idea what they would be.) Well, mathematics allows for additional dimensions which our minds simply cannot properly envisage. Now, having blown your minds with that, we can move on.

Let's keep it simple and just think of the variables in three dimensions. The trains are running off all over the globe on different tracks separated by various angles (relationships) and we have drawn further lines between them all which represent the factors we are pulling out from the analysis. Let us take just one factor, and work out the angles between every variable and that factor. Some will be very close to it, and some will be far away. (Remember that we are talking about a range from 0 to 90 degrees in the geometry of it all.)

We can now attempt something called rotation. This shifts the pattern of tracks around to find the best fit of loadings around your factor. It usually maximises the high correlations and minimises the low ones. With the rotated matrix, we can start to figure out what the analysis is actually telling us. We now have (and SPSS will give you a table of these) a set of what are called *eigenvalues*. Eigenvalues tell you how much each variable loads on the factor. In other words, how close each track is to the best-fit track that we have built between them. In fact, eigenvalues represent the amount of variance explained by each factor. The total of all the eigenvalues adds up to the number of variables in the analysis, since the proportion of each variable explained by the combination of factors cannot exceed the number of variables there are! As a rule of thumb, factors with an eigenvalue of more than 1 are kept, and we regard such factors as meaningful. We then look at the variables which load on those factors, and try to name them, by thinking what each collection of variables has in common. This is exactly the same as when we said that violence and hatred have anger in common. This time, however, we might be looking for something that seven different items in a questionnaire have in common, or just two, or even 30. Statisticians cannot help you here. This is for you to work out. In the end, all the fancy number work simply leads you to a point at which you take over and use your common sense to name your factors. This is exactly the same situation as when you conduct any other statistical test. The formulae allow you to work out if one group is different from another, and so on, but SPSS will not work out for you a theory to fit your data. In the end, all the statistics take you only so far, and you must do the rest yourself.

Finally, I should point out that you can also have negative factor loadings. Interpret these just as you would negative correlations between variables. In fact, think back to when I told you that you could have trains running on the same track but in opposite directions.

This is only a brief introduction to the extremely complicated world of factor analysis. If you want to know more, many of the books in my Further Reading section will explain in more detail.

8

GOODNESS OF FIT AND CHI-SQUARED

The goodness-of-fit test is a particular test which deals with variables that all comprise nominal data. In its simplest form it can tell you whether a set of headcounts in different categories are significantly different from each other (for example it can tell you whether a voting poll giving Labour 30%, Conservatives 32% and Liberal Democrats 29% is telling you that there is a meaningful difference between the parties or if these figures are what you would expect by chance or if voting was to be decided by throwing coins over your shoulder into one of three buckets!) In fact, this simplest form of the goodness-of-fit test is something that you will be very unlikely to use. I don't ever remember needing to use it, except for the purposes of teaching about statistics. Therefore, we'll skip this basic form and move straight onto the more complicated version, which in itself is still rather easy to understand compared with many other inferential statistics.

Σ CHI-SQUARED

The chi-squared test is really a more sophisticated extension of the goodness-of-fit test. What makes it different is that it is able to cope with more than one variable at once, which also makes it a lot more useful to us.

It is rare that we need a basic goodness-of-fit test. Think about it: how often are you likely to need to know if the number of people behaving one way is greater than the number of people behaving in one or more other ways? How often do you want to know if 42 is bigger than 30 and 31? It is much more likely that you want to know if the proportion of one type of people behaving in a certain way depends upon some other factor. For instance, you might want to compare men and women using or not using umbrellas when out in the rain. A simple, one-way goodness of fit test could tell you if there were more men or women in your sample. It could also tell you if there were more umbrella users than non-users in your sample. However, it couldn't tell you if women are more likely to use umbrellas than men: the chi-squared can.

First of all, we must get straight the simple fact that chi-squared must be used only when we have headcounts of nominal data. Nothing else must be fed into this analysis, including percentages (although I have seen it done, unfortunately). So, chi-squared is only for analysing the total number of observations in various categories, such as men with umbrellas, men without umbrellas, women with umbrellas and women without. You count how many of each you see in a given time period, and that's the data. Chi-squared does the rest. So what does it do? It begins with a table of the things you have counted, and we call this a *contingency table*. In this context, a contingency is simply 'something that might happen'. We make a table with empty cells in it, and each cell represents something that might happen, such as a man carrying an umbrella. We don't know if it *will* happen, because we haven't collected the data yet, but we have to have a box to put the number in, if we do observe this particular behaviour. Table 8.1 is the contingency table with some data.

So, in our example, we collected data in the rain, by observing men and women passing by in a 1-hour period, and noted use of an umbrella. For example, 12 men were found using an umbrella. We call this particular version a 2×2 chi-squared, because there are two categories for each variable, i.e. sex and umbrella use both have two 'levels', if you like. The chi-squared formula now takes these data and chews them up to produce a single number, which we can compare against tables to check its value. We call this value chi-squared. The one question that most students cannot answer about chi-squared is exactly what a significant value of χ^2 means. Significant what? For such a basic test, taught so early on in a student's statistical career, it's amazing how little understood it is.

The way I find best describes the action of this particular statistical test is that it detects an asymmetry in the numbers in the cells. You will no doubt understand what symmetry means when it comes to physical objects. A square is symmetrical, because it is possible to fold it over, down

Table 8.1 A contingency table.

	Men	Women	Totals
With umbrella	12	23	35
Without umbrella	18	4	22
Totals	30	27	57

the middle, and the two halves will match exactly when they press against each other. Furthermore, a square is symmetrical in all planes, because it doesn't matter which way you fold it. You can fold it across the middle, down the middle, or diagonally, and you will still get a perfect match between the two halves. A circle is also perfectly symmetrical. However, it is also possible to have symmetry on some planes but not others. For example, an equilateral triangle is symmetrical in the vertical plane, but not others. Draw a line from the top point of an equilateral triangle down to the mid-point on the bottom edge. You can fold this perfectly over now. Unfortunately, you can't do this with a vertical bisection.

OK, so you understand physical symmetry. Have you ever thought that numbers in tables can also be symmetrical? If I write four 5s in a 2×2 table, as above, you can fold it vertically, and two 5s will touch two 5s. If I fold it horizontally, then again two 5s touch two 5s. In theory, it is actually perfectly symmetrical, since a diagonal fold means that the top left 5 touches the bottom right 5, *and* each of the other two cells is cut in two by the fold. Therefore, effectively, 2.5 touches 2.5 each time. Are you still following me? If not, try this for real on a piece of paper, and look at those areas of the cells that I claim have a *theoretical* 2.5 in them. (Note that this doesn't necessarily work for complicated tables, like 3×3, where you can't really make the folds in the right way!).

Now, the next thing for you to understand is that the way that the chi-squared test detects asymmetry is not perfect. The numbers do not have to be completely asymmetrical, just near enough. 'Enough' is defined statistically too, but I won't worry you with exactly how. Suffice it to say that it's all to do with the probability of observing an asymmetry if there isn't really one in nature. The closer the numbers get to each other, the more likely you are to observe such a closeness by chance. The more the asymmetry, the smaller the possibility that your result is some kind of fluke.

Right now, we understand that chi-squared picks up asymmetry in the numbers in the cells, but we haven't got to the bit where we ask the obvious question. What do you compare the numbers in the cells with? All statistical tests involve a null hypothesis being tested against an alternative hypothesis, so where is the null hypothesis, as it were? Well, so far we have dealt only with what we call the observed frequencies. These are the numbers actually in the cells, the headcounts, and so on. We need to compare these with what would happen if everything happened equally, with men and women behaving exactly the same when it comes to umbrella use in the rain. We call these the expected frequencies.

The expected frequencies are not what we expect to happen. After all, we have a hypothesis to chase, and we truly expect an asymmetry, with men being different from women, or whatever our study happens to be about. 'Expected' doesn't mean 'expected by us'. It means what we expect to happen if there's no difference between men and women, fish and frogs, or whatever.

Now, you'd naturally be forgiven for thinking that calculating the expected frequencies is easy. After all, if there's no difference between the occurrence of X and the occurrence of Y, and the occurrence of P and Q, then surely you'd expect a 50:50 distribution? Therefore, a quarter of the observations should go in each of the four cells. This is true, and perfectly symmetrical, but it is rarely what happens when we calculate expected frequencies. This happens only when we observe exactly the same number of men and women and the same number of umbrella users and non-users. But, life being life, we usually don't. Therefore, we end up with different observed frequencies across categories of behaviour. We must, therefore, calculate the expected frequencies cell by cell, taking into account the unequal observation sizes. We usually can't just divide the total number of observations by four (in the case of a 2×2 of course).

For those of you who can easily follow formulae, we calculate the expected values thus:

$$E = \frac{R \times C}{T}$$

If you don't comprehend formulae that well, don't panic. As long as you understand the idea of working out expected frequencies and comparing them with observed frequencies, you have understood 90% of what chi-squared is about.

Now, the asymmetry I wrote about previously comes back into play. Although the formulae for chi-squared compares observed frequencies with expected ones, essentially you can interpret the results by looking only at the contingency table and seeking out any obvious discrepancies. In our umbrella example, you can see that, when it rains, men are more likely to not have an umbrella than to have one, whereas the opposite trend occurs for women. This is an example of what I mean by asymmetry. However you fold the table, like doesn't touch like. In the real world, you often don't often see things this clearly, so be ready to look carefully at a contingency table if you have a significant value of chi-squared. Can you imagine how difficult this could be if you were looking at a 4×4 contingency table? Knowing that at least one of the numbers is statistically not like the others doesn't really help much when you are looking at a matrix of 16 cells, none of which are actually identical. Let this be a lesson: stick to small contingency tables.

I can now tell you that chi-squared is also something that you can imagine as a correlation that has been collapsed down. Essentially, we want to know if being a man or a woman correlates in a particular way with carrying an umbrella. In fact, we can express chi-squared in the form of a correlation coefficient, the phi coefficient, which you will find elsewhere in this book. It is also remarkably similar to a test of interaction in ANOVA.

Earlier, I told you that you must only use raw counts in the cells of a contingency table for analysis by chi-squared. There are other things to consider when you intend using this method of analysis, which are very important.

Chi-squared assumes *independence of observations* in cells. You must never break this assumption. You're probably quite willing to stick to this rule, but you might need me to explain what independence of observations actually means! Basically, each observation should appear in only one cell. In fact, it shouldn't be possible for a person to pop up in more than one cell, if you like. Therefore, at any given point in time, as far as the observations made go, men are men and women are women. A man must not also appear in the women's cells and vice versa. This is unlikely, I admit. However, at the point of observation, each person must be only with an umbrella or without an umbrella. Of course, you might point out that it's hard to be anything else. The issue here is that you must clearly define what you count as umbrella use and what you don't. Furthermore, you must not count the same person twice. If a woman walks past using an umbrella, and then comes back without one, that poses a problem for you. Another example might be asking people to choose soups that they like. Doing this breaks the assumption because people might choose more than one soup, thus appearing in more than one cell of the contingency table. You can get around this by asking people to name their *favourite* soup. In this case, they are allowed only one, because that's what the word 'favourite' implies.

Another problem you must be aware of is the size of expected frequency cells. If an expected frequency for a cell is too low, the chi-squared analysis will not work properly. You are probably wondering how low is too low, and this is a topic of some debate amongst statisticians. For most of your work, you will be dealing with only 2×2 contingency tables, and generally no more than 3×3. Beyond this, the results become very difficult to interpret anyway. As a rule of thumb, try to avoid situations in which you end up with expected frequencies fewer than about three per cell, and aim for at least five (I am averaging over the advice given by other statisticians here).

If you have a large enough sample size, you are probably safe anyway, and by large I mean more than 20 observations in total. For most small projects, this is easy to achieve. Observations often yield hundreds of examples in a very short time. Another tip is to completely avoid collecting data on something that hardly ever happens. If necessary, collapse categories. So, if you are looking to spot people wearing hats of different colours, don't set out five categories such as white, yellow, green, blue and black. You must ask yourself how many people you are likely to spot wearing a yellow hat, for example. Consider rethinking your design so that, perhaps, you collect data on only light-coloured and dark-coloured hats, giving just two categories and plenty of observations for each.

Σ DEGREES OF FREEDOM

Most statistical tests that you encounter will have a measure of degrees of freedom (df) associated with them. Much of the time, you are simply told to make a note of this, or give details of the df in the reporting of the statistical tests, often without understanding what df are. This was the case when I was first taught psychological statistics. They were a mysterious thing that we had to know what to do with without really knowing what they were.

The first thing to realise is that 'degrees of freedom' really ought to be 'degrees of freedom of measurement'. Measurement is what the opaque phrase 'degrees of freedom' refers to. So what do we mean by degrees of freedom to measure something? Well, there are many ways I can try to explain this to you, and I'm going to try them all, because what works for one person doesn't work for another. Bear with me if you happen to understand this first time around.

Let me ask you a question. Are you taller? Now, you don't know what I mean, do you? Taller than whom? Basically, you need a point of comparison to measure something. Are you taller than you used to be? Are you taller than your friend? Suddenly, the question makes sense. We can take this a stage further. Imagine that you have a tape measure. If I were to ask you to measure the height of your best friend, what would you do? I happen to know that not everyone reading this will have thought the same thing. A proportion of you would have put the tape measure at the top of the head of the person involved, and then run it straight down to the floor. The remainder would have put the tape under the foot and pulled it up to the top of the head. Both methods, of course, are entirely legitimate. It doesn't matter whether you start from the top or the bottom: the measurement

STATISTICIANS LIKE TO
PRACTISE TAI CHI-SQUARED
TO RELAX....

will be the same. But, remember that you must start *somewhere*. When you do this, the start of the tape measure is a *fixed point of measurement*. The actual height of the person is free to vary, depending on how tall they are, which in itself depends upon heredity, nutrition, and so on. So, we have a fixed point of measurement, and, if you like, one degree of freedom.

Another way to look at this is the dinner table analogy. If I am holding a dinner party, and I invite seven people, there will be eight in total, including myself. I'm going to let people sit where they like. Once they have all arrived, and are seated, I ask one of them to leave the room. I sit down too. Then I call in my neighbour, and tell her to spot where my friend Neil was sitting. Of course, there is one seat empty, and so she can point to it. However, what would happen if I had asked two guests to leave the room, and then brought the neighbour in and asked the same question? Now there are two empty chairs, and thus two possibilities for Neil's seat, and no way of working out, from the information available, which is which; it's now impossible to complete the equation because there are too many unknowns. This is how degrees of freedom work. In this case, there are 7 degrees of freedom, because you need seven bits of information to work out the eighth.

When we compare the scores of two groups of people, for instance using an independent t-test, we effectively fix the mean of one set and use that as the comparison with the mean of the other set. It doesn't matter which group we use as our reference point, but we have to use one. It's more complicated than this, however. We now need to think of degrees of freedom in a slightly different way. In statistical terms, we need to imagine what we would need to know to calculate a person's score if we had the means of each set, and we knew how many people were in each. If you think back to basic algebra, you will remember that you can't solve equations with too many unknowns. If I have the mean of a set of scores, and know how many scores are in the set, I can calculate one score if I don't know it. I can't calculate two. You can try this with some sample data if you like, but alternatively you can simply trust me. Of course, this gives a df of $N - 1$. That is, the sample size minus the one score you don't know (don't forget that you also need the mean). In a set of 10 scores, the df would be 9. In case I have lost you, let's try the simplest example possible. I have a mean of 1, and two scores in the set. I know that one score is 1.5. The other score can be worked out as 0.5. Now, in the case of an independent t-test, we actually have two sets of scores. Therefore, the degrees of freedom for such a test is actually the total of the two sample sizes minus 2. We can work out two missing numbers (provided, of course, than only one comes from each set).

You should, at this point, be able to guess what the degrees of freedom for a related *t*-test are. This time, we have just one group of people, tested or measured twice. The test is based upon a difference score, that is, we make just one score out of two by subtracting one from the other for each person. So we end up with one set of scores. It's obvious, then, that the df is now just $N - 1$. In other words, we could calculate one missing score from the set of difference scores if we knew how many there were, and what the mean was. In other words, we'd need *all of the scores but one*, plus the mean, to calculate the missing score.

OK, so what happens in a correlation, like the Pearson's product moment coefficient? In this case, we have two sets of scores from the same people, but we don't calculate a difference score, because we are looking at relationships, not differences. So, two sets remain. This means that we are in a position similar to that of the independent *t*-test. Therefore, the df is the same $(N - 2)$. It really is that simple.

DEGREES OF FREEDOM...

Table 8.2 Contingency data for drink choice in men and women.

	Men	Women	Totals
Beer	50	8	58
Wine	9	54	63
Totals	59	62	121

There are many other tests, of course, and they all have their particular calculations of degrees of freedom. At this stage, I want to tell you about just one more: the chi-squared test. It's a nice way to finish this chapter, I think.

In this case, you end up with data in a contingency table, with row and column totals, as in Table 8.2. Here, we have asked men and women to state their outright favourite drink from either beer or wine. The numbers in the cells represent how many men and women chose each.

OK, this time, instead of means, think column and row totals. So, we have four numbers, and the column totals. How many missing numbers could we work out if we had all of the column and row totals? The answer is three. If we knew just one of these four cell counts, we could work the others out. This is what the df calculation for chi-squared works out for us, although it looks a bit complicated at first, because it is $Nc - 1$ multiplied by $Nr - 1$. There are two rows, and two columns, so that's 1 times 1, giving us 1. So, with a 3×3 chi-squared test, the df is 4. We'd need four out of the nine cells to calculate what the others would logically have to be. In the case of a 12×12 chi-squared, the df is 121, and so on.

9

NON-PARAMETRIC TESTS

Non-parametric tests are the best thing since sliced bread. Not quite true, but they are really very useful, either because the data we are collecting are never going to be normally distributed because they naturally don't occur that way or because for some reason our data are slightly 'wonky' and we really don't want to start again or give up completely.

There are many non-parametric tests, and there tends to be a non-parametric 'cousin' for every parametric test. They are called non-parametric because they can cope with data outside of the parameters that are required by the other tests (i.e. the parametric ones). Basically, they are not as fussy about what they eat. You have to be very careful what you feed your parametric pets, but non-parametric tests are like goats. They'll chew on just about anything. Of course, this then makes you wonder why we bother with the fussy old parametric tests. There's a great reason; parametric tests are extremely sensitive. If a difference exists, a parametric test is highly likely to show it to you. If a relationship between variables exists, a parametric correlation is fairly good at detecting it. Non-parametric tests are nowhere near as sensitive. They miss things. They are usually based on ranked data, and this in itself solves one problem whilst creating another. The ranking is a kind of transformation that removes outliers, but it also has the property of removing some of the very variance in scores that you need to demonstrate a difference that might exist.

Take these numbers: 2, 3, 5, 6, 8, 9. If you rank them, you get 1, 2, 3, 4, 5, 6. Now, if I stick an outlier in, we might have 2, 3, 5, 6, 8, 200. The ranks stay the same: 1, 2, 3, 4, 5, 6. That might be a good thing, you could say. However, now let us take the next step, which is the principle on which non-parametric tests of difference work. They involve ranking all the data together, not in separate groups. Look at the table of scores from two conditions (Table 9.1). I have given the raw scores and the ranked scores in each case, so that you can compare them.

Can you see what has happened? The mean score of the second condition is more than four times that of the first (4.69 to be more exact), whereas when the scores are ranked the difference is effectively squashed down, so that 126 is only 2.8 times 45. We've enabled those outlying scores (the 48 and 58 in the second condition) to be silenced, but in doing so we have lost some of the difference. This is the main reason why non-parametric tests are less sensitive than parametric ones. Bear that in mind.

Σ MANN–WHITNEY U-TEST

The Mann–Whitney U-test is the non-parametric 'cousin' of the independent t-test. It is, therefore, used for ordinal data (or data which may be interval or ratio but is not normally distributed) collected from two different groups of people. Like other non-parametric tests, it is based on ranks, which means that the scores are turned into ordinal data, which loses some information but at least allows us to make inferences just as we do with the parametric equivalents. If you calculate Mann–Whitney U by hand, which you won't have to do thanks to SPSS and other, similar, software, you calculate the ranks in a particular way which involves a system of comparing each number with the numbers in the other group. It doesn't matter how big the difference between them is, but simply that there is a difference at all. If the difference exists, and that difference applies to most numbers in a systematic way, then you'll pick up a significant difference between groups. By systematic, I simply mean that scores in group A will have to be bigger than scores in group B (*or vice versa*) consistently, or time and time again. If the scores are different, the ranks are different. If

Table 9.1 Data and ranks.

Condition 1 raw scores	Condition 2 raw scores	Condition 1 ranks	Condition 2 ranks
1	10	1	10
2	12	2	11
3	13	3	12
4	14	4	13
5	15	5	14
6	16	6	15
7	25	7	16
8	48	8	17
9	58	9	18
Mean = 5	Mean = 23.44	Rank sum = 45	Rank sum = 126

the ranks are different, you will probably find that the distance between them is significant.

Σ WILCOXON RANK-SUM TEST

This is a common, non-parametric version of independent t, just like the Mann–Whitney U. Just to confuse you it has a very similar name to the other famous test developed by Wilcoxon, the matched-pairs signed-rank test, which you will find below. Not only that, but when you calculate the rank-sum test statistic, you get a figure which is simply a mathematical variant of the Mann–Whitney U. You can easily convert one to the other if you have the right constant. For that reason, I won't say any more about the Wilcoxon rank-sum test.

Σ WILCOXON MATCHED-PAIRS SIGNED-RANK TEST

The Wilcoxon matched-pairs signed-rank test is the non-parametric equivalent of a related t test. You can remember this easily because Wilcoxon begins with W, and it is used for within-groups designs (as is the related t). The calculation for Wilcoxon basically involves taking the difference between each pair of scores. The logic is that, as each pair comes from one person, the difference tells you almost as much as the scores in the pair. At this point, however, you need to bear in mind that some of those differences could be positive and some negative. Then, the differences are ranked, temporarily ignoring the pluses and minuses. We then separate the ranks for the minuses and the ranks for the pluses, and we add up each set to give us two sums of ranks (which is why the test gets this name). The fundamental principle here is that if the original scores are not different then the sums of ranks of the scores won't be different either. You are probably wondering why we bother ranking them in the first place. Why not take the original scores? Well, the answer is complicated, and not something this book is intended to teach you, but the main reason is that ranks are like a transformation of the data. The whole point of using a non-parametric test is because your data are not normally distributed, and there could be some wild, outlying, extreme numbers in there. Ranking numbers reduces that problem.

Σ SPEARMAN'S RHO

This is a non-parametric correlation. That's really all you need to know. SPSS will happily compute both Pearson's R and Spearman's rho at the same time, so you can compare them. It's not a bad idea to do this, because if they give you very different correlation coefficients you might want to look carefully at your data, since there might be something amiss. It is often a sign that you have not met the assumptions of the parametric test of correlation (i.e. Pearson's R), and so you may be better accepting the non-parametric version instead.

Σ KRUSKAL–WALLIS

The Kruskal–Wallis test is used when we can't use an unrelated (between-groups) one-way ANOVA. So, when we want to detect a trend of difference across three or more groups of scores, and those scores don't meet parametric test requirements, the Kruskal–Wallis will do the trick. It is pretty much the same as a set of Wilcoxon rank-sum tests stuck together, just like the between-groups ANOVA is a kind of gluing together of independent t-tests. Follow this up with Mann–Whitney U-tests with a Bonferroni correction when you want to conduct *post-hoc* analysis.

Σ FRIEDMAN'S RANK TEST

This is the within-groups non-parametric equivalent of one-way ANOVA. It is therefore the best friend of the Kruskal–Wallis test. In fact, it is largely the same as the repeated-measures one-way ANOVA worked out on ranked scores instead of the originals. Follow this up with Wilcoxon matched-pairs tests with a Bonferroni correction when you want to run *post-hoc* analysis to find exactly where a significant effect lies.

10

RARELY USED TESTS IN THE SEEDY UNDERBELLY OF STATISTICS

In this chapter I hope to make you familiar with the lesser used, but actually very handy, statistical tests (many of which are essentially non-parametric too). It is not uncommon for students (and some researchers) to end up with data which they are not sure how to analyse, and in fact sometimes those data are, for the most part, un-analysable. However, a knowledge of some of the rarer tests can often save the day, by allowing at least some inferential statistical manipulation of the data. Of course, the tests in this chapter should not be seen as purely intended for emergency purposes. They are actually tests in their own right developed for specific reasons, and technically they deserve the same amount of respect and appropriate use as other tests. However, the nature of these tests is such that it is relatively rare for someone to design a study around them as the planned analysis, partly because they use strange forms of data, and partly because they can be a little too basic for most researchers' requirements. You never know when you might need them, however, and most beginners' books miss them out, so you can regard this chapter as a little treat. (Sometimes my sarcasm gets the better of me.)

Σ KENDALL'S TAU

This is a non-parametric correlation coefficient which can be seen as a rival to Spearman's rho. Instead of being based on simple rankings, it is based on what we call *inversions* of the rankings. I rank both my columns then I take one of my groups and put them in order of rank, with the first at the top and the last at the bottom. Then I count, for each rank in the other group, the number of times a rank is bigger in that column but below it. This is best shown in an example in Table 10.1.

The logic is that if two variables are highly positively correlated, there

Table 10.1 Ranked data and Inversions for Kendall's tau

Rank A	Rank B	Inversions
1	1	0
2	3	1
3	8	5
4	5	2
5	2	0
6	10	4
7	9	3
8	7	2
9	4	0
10	6	0

should be very few inversions, because low ranks in one should go with the low ranks in the other, and vice versa. If they are highly negatively correlated, there will be a high number of inversions. If they are not correlated at all, the inversions will be moderate, essentially. To work out Kendall's tau, you multiply the number of inversions by two, then divide by the number of possible pairs and take all of this away from 1. The number of possible pairs is given by $N(N-1)/2$, so with 10 pairs of rankings, as in the above example, there are 45 pairs (10×9 divided by 2). There are 17 inversions in the above data, so the value of tau would be approximately 0.25.

Σ THE SIGN TEST

The sign test (also called the binomial sign test) is a handy way to determine if scores have changed. It is used primarily on ordinal data (especially when they are technically ordinal but might appear as if they are interval data), and is simply a way of counting up the number of positive and negative changes that occur from the first point in time to the second. The logic is that if scores are consistently higher at point B than point A, then there will be a lot of plus signs when we calculate the differences, whereas if just as many scores rise as fall there will be an equal number of plus and minus signs. The proportion of plus signs can be tested as to its likelihood of occurring if the null hypothesis is true. That is, if in the real world one would end up with a perfect split of plus and minus signs, one can also determine how likely or unlikely 70% pluses would be, or 99% pluses, and so on. Of course, there are a few things to consider. What do you do when there is a zero instead of a plus or minus, that is when there is no change? Well, essentially, you don't count it. The sign test can't really deal with them. So, if we start with 100 pairs of scores, but 35 of them don't change, then we throw those out and pretend that they were not there. Instead, we base all of our sign test calculations on 65 pairs of scores. We don't worry about the size of the difference either. The sign test is not about numbers, but about directions of difference. If B is higher then A, then it doesn't matter how much higher. We simply count how many positive differences we have, and how many negative differences, and then we choose the smallest of those two numbers, which becomes the observed value that we are interested in. We then look that up in a table of S (the sign test statistic), and if our small number is smaller than the one in the table we assume significance. We might simply let our software calculate an exact probability for us, of course.

Σ THE BINOMIAL TEST

Imagine that we have a room full of people. Some of them have the middle name 'Frank'. I have to try to guess which ones. Therefore, I separate them out into two groups depending on whether or not I believe they have Frank as their middle name. Then, the answers are revealed. Effectively then, I can count the number of times I was right and the number of times I was wrong. How do I know if I was operating purely at chance level, or if I was better than chance at detecting Franks? The binomial test, which you can find on the menus of SPSS, will do this calculation.

Σ POINT-BISERIAL CORRELATION COEFFICIENT

This is a strange test for a couple of reasons, and because of that you are unlikely to use it, but I am telling you about it because it actually is a good way to get across a completely different point, which is the relationship between correlation and difference tests.

The point-biserial (known as r_{pb}) is a way of correlating a dichotomous variable with a continuous one, that is a variable that has only two outcomes (such as male/female, young/old, blonde/non-blonde) with a variable which has many possible outcomes along some dimension (such as height, angling expertise, number of insects per square metre, and so on). The strange thing is that although a dichotomous variable is clearly suited to a non-parametric test, the point-biserial correlation coefficient involves using Pearson's *r*, which as you know is a parametric test. Without going into the long-winded reason for this, suffice it to say that if you use the wrong test it can sometimes serve a different purpose quite well, and this is how the point-biserial works. If you wrongly use a parametric test, because you don't know what you are doing, then this is inexcusable. If, however, you use it carefully because it *can* do the job you want as long as you understand what you are doing, then this is a different story altogether.

The problem is that there's arguably no good reason to do this most of the time. Here's the important bit. If you correlate a bunch of 1s and 2s with a continuous variable, you end up with a correlation coefficient that is basically the same thing as a difference test in disguise. Think about it. Look at the data in Table 10.2. Hopefully, you can see that really these look more like data that feed into a difference test than a correlation. If we compute a correlation on this, then a significant relationship would tell us that the number of flamingos seen is correlated with sex. That's just a strange way of saying that the number of flamingos seen is significantly different between men and women. So, the argument would be that a difference test is more suitable. So, this is why you might never use the point-biserial correlation coefficient. It is useful to know it exists though, because it shows you how correlations and difference tests are really from the same family, and, in fact, the point-biserial correlation can be converted to a *t*-value quite easily, giving you the same thing as if you had worked out *t* in the first place.

Table 10.2 Data fitting a point-biserial correlation coefficient.

Sex	Number of flamingos seen in lifetime
1	14
1	15
1	12
1	10
1	22
2	31
2	8
2	11
2	11
2	10

Σ THE BISERIAL CORRELATION COEFFICIENT

This is the close friend of the point-biserial, and is pretty much the same thing, except that one of your variables is dichotomous only because you made it that way, even though it needn't be. What do I mean by this? Well, imagine that you took a set of scores that were normally distributed. Age is a good example, and one that commonly gets compressed in this way. If we decided to convert age into two groups, 'young' and 'old', ignoring the actual values, then we would have forced a normally distributed variable into a dichotomy. This is just the kind of variable that the biserial is set up to work on. I won't give you the formula for it, which you can get elsewhere. Anyway, I don't want to encourage you to use this for a number of reasons: (a) you should use it only when you are certain that the underlying dimension is normally distributed, (b) you should have started with a continuous variable in the first place instead of losing sensitivity by allowing yourself to work with a dichotomous one, and (c) it's complicated to work out and you might not like it anyway.

Σ THE PHI COEFFICIENT

This is the correlation to use when you are dealing with two dichotomous variables. However, you must have what might be called 'true' dichotomies. By this I mean that the two outcomes for each variable should be the only outcomes possible in normal circumstances, as in the case of male/female and university-educated/not university educated. I say 'normal circumstances' because technically male/female is not a true dichotomy, although it tends to be accepted as such. We can argue over the politics of this, because as you will be aware there are people who have characteristics of both sexes and doctors argue over what sex they really are. I wouldn't want to ignore that these people exist by glibly saying that there is only male and female, although again some biologists would say that the chromosomes give it away regardless of the outward appearance. However, I'm moving away from statistics, so I'll come back to the point. With two dichotomous variables, you use the phi coefficient (the symbol for phi is this: Φ). The phi coefficient, however, is again an example where we calculate a Pearson's r even though it's a bit sneaky, and then convert that value to a chi-squared. In fact, you hopefully noticed that with two dichotomous variables you have a design which matches exactly what you would have for a 2×2 chi-squared. All of this begs the question why you'd bother at all. Why not just calculate a 2×2 chi-squared in the first place and have done with it? Ninety-nine per cent of the time that's what you'd do, and let's leave it at that.

Σ McNEMAR'S TEST AND COCHRAN'S *Q*

As you will remember, the chi-squared coefficient is set up to work only when the outcomes are independent. That is, when the possible answers cannot overlap, or observations cannot appear in more than one cell. People must be one thing or another, or give mutually exclusive answers like 'yes' or 'no', and this effectively means that you always use this where you have a kind of between-groups design. What happens when you need to compare proportions of 'yes' responses and 'no' responses, or any other binary response, when you have a within-groups design, such as you get with 'before' and 'after'? The answer is that you use these two tests. The McNemar is the simper version, and in fact a 2×2 Cochran's *Q* is really just a McNemar. Imagine that you wanted to test the effects of a drug on someone's general health. You are measuring health very crudely, such as with two terms, 'good' or 'bad'. You get health ratings before and after the drug is administered, giving you a total of four cells in your observation, which correspond to 'good before', 'bad before', 'good after', 'bad after'. The McNemar will tell you if there is a change in the proportion of goods to bads before and after. It is effectively a version of chi-squared. For more complicated versions, with additional responses, a Cochran's *Q* can be performed.

Clark-Carter (2004) tells you how to use them and calculate them (unlike most books, which never mention either).

Σ COHEN'S KAPPA

Cohen's kappa is a test used in observational studies in which you need to be sure that two raters have strong agreement. It's a test of inter-rater reliability. Furthermore, it's technically not an inferential statistical test, which I suppose means that it should not be in this book at all. However, let us not concern ourselves with technicalities! The test is useful, and you might need it, especially if you decide to conduct observational research for a project, so it is worth describing here.

Imagine that two different and independent people have watched a recording of children playing and have classified their play into three types: violent, compassionate or neutral. When the children hit each other or objects, the play is said to be violent. When they show signs of co-operation or empathy with others, the play is compassionate. When neither occurs, we call it neutral. Now although this seems straightforward, it might not always be. We need to be sure that the play is properly coded, and that's why we have two independent raters. What would you do if you saw a child hit an object because the object had just fallen on her friend and hurt her? The violent act is actually a compassionate one, so what do we do? Well, we see what the raters make of it, and hope that they agree. Now, we could just do this by means of percentage agreement. In fact, this is possibly just what we would do if there were only two categories of response, for example 'yes' and 'no'. Things are more complicated here though, and so Cohen's kappa saves the day. The reason it is important to go further than percentage agreement is that you would expect some agreement by chance alone. Even if there is a 90% agreement, you have to consider that when there are only two categories of response two monkeys would agree half of the time! Similarly, with three categories, the chance agreement would be 33%.

At the end of your hypothetical study, you have a series of events, and each event is coded by each rater as 1, 2 or 3, or V, C or N. We can plot the ratings for each observer in a 3×3 table, just like a 3×3 chi-squared contingency table actually (Table 10.3).

The important part of this table is the agreement, and this is to be found in the diagonals. Add these numbers up, and you end up with 8, 7 and 6, giving you 21. We therefore have 21 agreements out of 32, which is actually almost 66%. The next step is to work out what would have happened in these cells of the table by chance alone. This is almost exactly what you do in a normal chi-squared calculation, except this time we are interested only in the diagonals; the rest do not matter. To calculate the expected frequencies we simply multiply the row total by the column total, and divide by the overall total of all observations (32 in our case). This gives us for 4.5 for VV agreement, 3.75 for CC agreement and 2.5 for NN agreement. We add these up to give us 10.75.

Table 10.3 A 3×3 contingency table.

	V	C	N	Totals
V	8	2	2	12
C	3	7	2	12
N	1	1	6	8
Totals	12	10	10	32

Take the total of the expected frequencies in the diagonals away from the total observed in the diagonals, i.e. 21 – 10.75, which is 10.25. Next, take the expected total away from the number of observations, i.e. 32 – 10.75, which is 21.25. All we have to do know is divide the 10.25 by the 21.25. This is our value of kappa, which is 0.48. We normally accept only values of kappa greater than 0.7, so in this case we cannot assume that the observers actually agree. In fact, although it's not quite correct to do so, you could imagine that the kappa is a percentage, that is 48%. Compare that with the 66% agreement that we noted earlier. But, remember what I said about chance agreements being taken into account. The 66% has been shifted down somewhat to allow for chance. As I said, it's not quite right to do this, but it certainly shows you why the percentage can't be relied on and kappa can.

Σ JONCKHEERE–TERPSTRA TEST

This test is included mainly because of the wonderful Dutch names that the inventors have, but also because every now and then it might be useful. Sometimes, it is called simply the Jonckheere's trend test. It is a further extension of the concept of a non-parametric one-way, between-groups ANOVA, but it is used where we have a particular directional hypothesis. What is meant by this is that we have, let us say, three groups that we expect to be ordered in some way. Normally we might hypothesise that there will be a difference between conditions X, Y and Z. What if we want to hypothesis that Z will be largest, followed by Y and then X. This time, we are predicting a much more specific outcome, and the Jonckheere–Terpstra will allow us to test this non-parametrically. A good example of where this might be used is in medical studies examining different dosages of a drug in different groups, or in psychological studies testing, for example, the results of 1 hour of training at a skill, 2 hours, or 3, where we are assuming that more training leads to greater demonstrable skill.

Σ PAGE'S L

Naturally you are now wondering what happens if you want to predict the ordering of scores from conditions, as with the Jonckheere–Terpstra, but this time you have a repeated measures design, that is the scores in each group come from the same people tested on different occasions. The answer is that you use Page's L. There isn't room to go into detail here, but if you really need the test I know you'll find out about it yourself. Looking for the detail is one of the best ways to learn more, which I really want to encourage you to do.

Σ WALD–WOLFOWITZ RUNS TEST

You are not particularly likely to need this test, but I think you should try saying it out loud. It's interesting on the ear, I think. Basically, this is a kind of test of randomness. It works out whether sequences (or runs) in your data are too consistent to be put down to randomicity. As you will know, random sequences can have runs in them, but too many runs start to look like there's something else going on.

Compare these two 'random' sequences of coin tosses (H is heads, and T is tails, just in case you are drifting off):

HHTHTHTTHHHTTHTTHTHHTTHT
TTTHHHTTTTTTTTHTTTHTTTTT

The first looks quite likely, whereas the second looks as if we might have a coin that is biased. The Wald–Wolfowitz will detect unusual runs, like the predominance of tails in the second sequence. You can find this test in SPSS.

Σ FABJICK'S *P*-TEST

OK, I made this one up. It is the end of the book, after all. But, if you ever become a statistician and get to create your own test and publish it, try to remember this, and if Fabjick's *P* ever turns up somewhere else, I'll be very pleased.

REFERENCES

Coolican, H. (2004) *Research Methods and Statistics in Psychology*, 4th edn. London: Hodder & Stoughton.

Dancey, C.P. and Reidy, J. (2002) *Statistics Without Maths for Psychology: Using SPSS for Windows*, 2nd edn. Harlow: Pearson Prentice Hall.

Howell, D.C. (2007) *Statistical Methods for Psychology*, 6th edn. Belmont, CA: Thomson Wadsworth.

Tabachnik, B.G. and Fidell, L.S. (1996) *Using Multivariate Statistics*, 3rd edn. New York: HarperCollins.

FURTHER READING

The following books are those I recommend for further reading. They are all suited to moving onto once you have read this book. I have divided them into three phases. The first phase consists of books that will take you into similar territory as this book, and a little further. The second phase contains books that go beyond phase 1, and phase 3 books are for dipping into for much more detail. This is only my opinion, however, and it wouldn't hurt to read any book on statistics at any point in your career as a psychological statistician. Remember not to be afraid. If you don't understand something, it doesn't mean that you never will. Everyone has to start somewhere. There was a time when all the people who wrote books on statistics knew nothing about the subject. Most of them probably taught themselves, by reading, and thinking about what they were reading, and asking questions.

Σ PHASE 1

Jackson, S.L. (2006) *Research Methods and Statistics: a Critical Thinking Approach*, 2nd edn. Belmont, CA: Thomson Wadsworth.
Miles, J. (2001) *Research Methods and Statistics*. Exeter: Crucial.

Σ PHASE 2

Clark-Carter, D. (2004) *Quantitative Psychological Research: A Student's Handbook*. Hove: Psychology Press.
Coolican, H. (2004) *Research Methods and Statistics in Psychology*, 4th edn. London: Hodder & Stoughton.
Dancey, C.P. and Reidy, J. (2002) *Statistics Without Maths for Psychology: Using SPSS for Windows*, 2nd edn. Harlow: Pearson Prentice Hall.
Field, A. (2005) *Discovering Statistics Using SPSS*, 2nd edn. London: Sage.

Langdridge, D. (2004) *Introduction to Research Methods and Data Analysis in Psychology.* Harlow: Pearson Prentice Hall.

Σ PHASE 3

Howell, D.C. (2004) *Fundamental Statistics for the Behavioural Sciences*, 5th edn. Belmont, CA: Duxbury Press.

Howell, D.C. (2007) *Statistical Methods for Psychology*, 6th edn. Belmont, CA: Thomson Wadsworth.

Keppel, G. (1991) *Design and Analysis: a Researcher's Handbook*, 3rd edn. Englewood Cliffs, NJ: Prentice Hall.

Siegel, S. and Castellan, N.J. (1988) *Nonparametric Statistics for the Behavioural Sciences*, 2nd edn. London: McGraw-Hill.

INDEX